Restoring the

FIVEFOLD MINISTRY

SECOND EDITION

Avoiding the Pastoral
Supremacy Syndrome

Hartwell Paul Davis

ISBN 978-1-0980-0808-6 (paperback)
ISBN 978-1-0980-0809-3 (digital)

Christian Faith Publishing, Inc.
832 Park Avenue
Meadville, PA 16335
www.christianfaithpublishing.com

Printed in the United States of America

CONTENTS

Foreword..5

Chapter 1—Introduction 7

Chapter 2—So You Want to Be a Preacher 15

Chapter 3—The First Mega Church 29

Chapter 4—Organizational Identity..32

Chapter 5—Christians on the Broadway 46

Chapter 6—Church Polity 57

Chapter 7—Power Structures 64

Chapter 8—The Earliest Power Structures 72

Chapter 9—Leadership Development 83

Chapter 10—The Called, Chosen, and Faithful Leader...............96

Chapter 11—The Called Leader 100

Chapter 12—The Chosen Leader 103

Chapter 13—The Faithful Leader 110

Chapter 14—Maladaptive Church Leadership 115

Chapter 15—Avoiding the Pastoral Supremacy Syndrome 124

Chapter 16—The Awakening...138

Chapter 17—The Fivefold Ministry..148

Chapter 18—The Apostle 151

Chapter 19—The Prophet 155

Chapter 20—The Evangelist 159

Chapter 21—The Pastor and Elders 161

Chapter 22—Teacher 169
Chapter 23—The Ministry of Women 171
Chapter 24—Restoration Leadership 177

Bibliography 185

FOREWORD

In 2004 I published my first book, *Restoring the Fivefold Ministry*, as a treatise of lessons learned as a church planter, evangelist, and pastor over a period of forty years. Not only have these many lessons from the school of hard knocks challenged me as a Christian, but they also challenged me as a preacher and as a pastor. By preacher, I am speaking about a person who assumes the role of an "oracle of truth." The definition of *oracle* is a priest or priestess through whom a deity is believed to speak, or a person who delivers authoritative, wise, or highly regarded and influential pronouncements (*Merriam-Webster*). In ancient Greece, an oracle was synonymous with prophet or prophetess.

If we dismiss the idea that the term *preacher* refers only to Christian preachers and understand the explicit definition, the term *preacher* could refer to anyone who communicates by sermons or homilies (including speeches, lectures, and discourses), a message, philosophy, or worldview intended to persuade an audience toward believing what is being communicated. One definition of *preach* is "to advocate earnestly" (*Merriam-Webster*), from the Latin *praedicare*, meaning to "make known." For example, Solomon speaks of himself as a preacher in Ecclesiastes, writing, "And moreover, because the preacher was wise, he still taught the people knowledge; yea, he gave good heed, and sought out, and set in order many proverbs" (Ecclesiastes 12:9, King James Version).

When a preacher assumes the role of an oracle of truth, it does not mean what is being said is true—it means the preacher wants the audience to believe it is true. Preachers exist in all educational, religious, or political contexts because each of these venues is about persuading people to believe the message espoused by the one doing the speaking. Religious preachers, along with politicians and educators, share a common thread in that the communication contains the philosophy and worldview of the speaker and the function of preaching is generally being done for the express purpose of sharing that worldview or philosophy.

This second edition of *Restoring the Fivefold Ministry* expands on the first edition by focusing on principles of church leadership. Included in the discussion is a conversation about one of the root causes of the misunderstanding that diminishes the role of fivefold ministry in the church: *the pastoral supremacy syndrome*. My own use of the term comes from research on its business cousin, founders syndrome, a term in the business world today to describe how entrepreneurs limit leadership in growing their organization by self-imposed centralized authority and symbolic power structures.

In addition to including text from *Restoring*, I have included in this book several chapters of my prior writings from my doctoral studies in leadership from Liberty University or Regent University. The chapter on "The Called, Chosen, and Faithful Leader" is published in the Education Resources Information Center as well as in Academia.edu and is included in full text.[1] The chapter on "Discipleship Methods" and an essay on "The Configuration of Servant Leadership"[2] are also included in full text. I will cite these in my reference page. Other than the ERIC published chapter, the other essays have not been formally published except to be uploaded on Academia, LinkedIn, or my own personal websites.

[1.] Hartwell Davis, "The Called, Chosen, and Faithful Leader" (2009). Retrieved from Education Resources Information Center, ED506263.

[2.] Hartwell Davis, "Power Structures in the Configuration of Servant Leadership," Essay for Organizational Leadership (Regent University, 2015).

CHAPTER 1

Introduction

"Take heed therefore unto your selves, and to all the flock, over the which the Holy Ghost hath made you overseers, to feed the church of God, which he hath purchased with his own blood" (Acts 20:28, KJV), Paul says to the elders of the Ephesian church whom he has called to Miletus for a final conference. In this one verse, Paul summarizes the basic duty of the spiritual ministry, which has oversight of God's flock. Guarding the flock and feeding the flock are the two main purposes of the overseer. But he precedes his instruction with a very strong admonition: "Take heed therefore unto your selves."

Jesus himself recognized that the shepherds of the flock were always great targets for Satan's devices. He quoted the prophet Zechariah: "Smite the shepherd, and the sheep shall be scattered" (Zechariah 13:7, Mark 14:27). Satan failed to smite the Great Shepherd with temptation and perhaps thought that death on Calvary would vanquish forever the Son of man. While the resurrection of Jesus Christ has proven forever that Satan is a defeated foe, it has not stopped this determined adversary from doing everything in his power to destroy the church of Jesus Christ. Satan did learn this one truth, however—that sheep will indeed flee when the shepherd is smitten. When a sheep is separated from the shepherd, he becomes prey.

This book deals with a different aspect of spiritual leadership. There have been books written by the score that deal with the sins of the ministry. The failures of some well-known preachers have only spotlighted facts that we should all know well: preachers are human and that a tall pedestal makes for a long fall. But the biggest reason for tragedy in ministry is not because of the personal sins of the individual minister but because the ministry itself has become something entirely different from that which God has ordained for his church.

First of all, preachers for the most part no longer minister. The calling of ministry has given way to the function of administration. If one wonders about why someone would want to become a bishop, elder, deacon, pastor—or whatever title one might choose—you have to ask the question, "Whose needs are being met?" The first principle of ministry is service, not to be served. When a vow of poverty includes the promise that your living will be generously provided, one has to wonder "whose needs are being met." If the "ministry" entails having the spotlight, "whose needs are being met?" When it is normal to receive the praise of men, "whose needs are being met?" All the basic temptations are inherent in being a preacher. Fame, fortune, prestige, the adoration of men or women, the chance to perform—all of these can be seen to flourish in the pulpit today. The most difficult problem of all is the fact that the position of minister in the scheme of things today is one of "authority." This was the very problem that Jesus warned about when he was defining the role of church leadership.

> But Jesus called them unto him, and said, Ye know that the princes of the Gentiles exercise dominion over them, and they that are great exercise authority upon them. But it shall not be so among you: but whosoever will be great among you, let him be your minister; And whosoever will be chief among you, let him be your servant: Even as the Son of man came not to be ministered unto, but to minister, and to give his life a ransom for many. (Matthew 20:25–28, KJV)

Jesus's basic pattern was authority inverted. How can this be? When we speak of church government, pastoral authority, ministerial leadership, and elders that rule, how do these things fit the idea of "minister"? It is impossible to understand the Lord's meaning if one looks at "authority" in its natural context and adopts the normal meaning of authority to this term. That is exactly why Jesus pointed out to his disciples that his way is not the way that the world sees authority. "It shall not be so among you," he said. The way to minister is as a servant.

When the Lord set up his kingdom, he established it with his principles of leadership in mind. For his model, he used not the model of a king as we know in Saul or David but the model of a servant. He actually used the model of a king dethroned, Moses, who fled the life of pleasure in the palaces of Egypt to tend to sheep in the desert. But since most preachers today believe that Moses was a type of pastor, it is very important to look deeply at the life of Moses to find exactly what shadow is being cast for the New Testament church.

Moses was not a type of pastor of the local church. Moses was a type of Jesus Christ and of Jesus Christ alone. He was a king who fled Egypt. This was a preview of the fulfilled prophecy of Jesus Christ spoken by Matthew: "And was there until the death of Herod: that it might be fulfilled which was spoken of the Lord by the prophet, saying, Out of Egypt have I called my son" (Matthew 2:15, KJV).

Moses, like Jesus, was condemned to death while still a child. His name means "drawn from the water." I find it interesting that Moses' mother did indeed obey the edict of Pharaoh to cast her son into the Nile River. However, she put an ark under him. Moses was spared by God's intervention, just as Jesus was spared by God's intervention. In many ways, we can find parallels in the life of Moses with the life of Christ. We know that Moses prophesied concerning Jesus Christ: "The LORD thy God will raise up unto thee a Prophet from the midst of thee, of thy brethren, like unto me; unto him ye shall hearken."

Moses was a king who became a shepherd. Jesus was a king who also became a shepherd. The Bible speaks of Jesus Christ as being our "chief Shepherd" (1 Peter 5:4), but it is this typology that has also been misunderstood. Many ministers today have taken Moses as a type of pastor of a local church rather than as a type of Jesus Christ, the one for whom this type was intended. Indeed, there is a type for the local pastors mentioned in the Old Testament. That type is elders. The elders of Moses, as recorded in Numbers 11, are a type of local pastors of the church insomuch as they are to receive the same spirit as their chief shepherd. Notice how this scripture reads:

> And the LORD came down in a cloud, and spake unto him, and took of the spirit that was upon him, and gave it unto the seventy elders: and it came to pass, that, when the spirit rested upon them, they prophesied, and did not cease. (Numbers 11:25)

In the course of this book, I hope to provide enough scripture to help the church to understand the principle of "eldership." The early church did not operate with a single person fulfilling an ecclesiastical role. There was no church with a pastor who had complete and total oversight of the local congregation. Instead there were only two offices that could be filled by elders from the local congregation or ordained by the apostles. These were the offices of elders and deacons (Philippians 1:1, 1 Timothy 3). It is important to understand that the office of elder (also known as "bishop" [Titus 1:5–7, 1 Timothy 3]) or deacon is distinct from the ministry of apostle, prophet, evangelist, pastor, and teacher. A pastor may be an elder, but not all elders have the ministry (or gift) of pastoring.

Quoting from the *International Standard Bible Encyclopedia* (1939) under the topic "Ministry," Lindsey writes,

> It may be said generally that about the close of the 1st century every Christian community was ruled by a body of men who are sometimes called presbyters (elders), sometimes but more rarely bishops (overseers), and whom modern church historians are inclined to call presbyter-bishops. Associated with them, but whether members of the same court or forming a court of their own

it is impossible to say, were a number of assistant rulers called deacons. The court of elders had no president or permanent chairman. There was a two-fold not a threefold ministry. During the 3rd century, rising into notice by way of geographical distribution rather than in definite chronological order, this twofold congregational ministry became threefold in the sense that one man was placed at the head of each community with the title of pastor or bishop (the titles are interchangeable as late as the 4th century at least). In the early centuries those local churches, thus organized, while they never lacked the sense that they all belonged to one body, were independent self-governing communities preserving relations to each other, not by any political organization embracing them all, but by fraternal fellowship through visits of deputies, interchange of letters, and in some indefinite way giving and receiving assistance in the selection and setting apart of pastors.[3]

Also,

The uniquely Christian correlation of the three conceptions of leadership, service and "gifts"; leadership depended on service, and service was possible by the possession and recognition of special "gifts," which were the evidence of the presence and power of the Spirit of Jesus within the community. The "gifts" gave the church a Divine

3. Thomas M. Lindsey, "Ministry: The Local Ministry," in *International Standard Bible Encyclopedia, 5th Edition (Online Edition)*, ed. James Orr (Grand Rapids, MI: William B. Eerdmans Publishing Company, 1939). Retrieved from https://www.internationalstandardbible.com/M/ministry.html.

authority to exercise rule and oversight apart from any special apostolic direction.[4]

Regarding the threefold congregational ministry, Lindsey writes,

> During the 2nd century the ministry was subject to a change. The ruling body of office-bearers in every congregation received a permanent president, who was called the pastor or bishop, the latter term being the commoner. The change came gradually. It provoked no strong opposition. By the beginning of the third century, it was everywhere accepted. When we seek to trace the causes why the college of elders received a president, who became the center of all the ecclesiastical life in the local church and the one potent office-bearer, we are reduced to conjecture. This only can be said with confidence, that the change began in the East and gradually spread to the West, and that there are hints of a gradual evolution.[5]

However, John Eadie (1875) writes that the early church father Jerome suggests that the reason for the elevation of one presbyter over others is that it was to resolve the division that was created by those who preferred Paul or Peter or Apollos (1 Corinthians 3:1–4). Eadie quotes Jerome, who wrote,

> A presbyter is the same as a bishop. And until, by the instigation of the devil, there arose divisions in religion, and it was said among the people, "I am of Paul, and I of Apollos, and I of Cephas," churches were governed by a common council of presbyters. But afterwards, when everyone

---

4. Lindsey, "Ministry: The Local Ministry."
5. Lindsey, "Ministry: Threefold Congregational Ministry."

> regarded those whom he baptized as belonging to himself rather than Christ, it was everywhere decreed, that one person, elected from the presbyters, should be placed over the others to whom the whole church might belong, and thus the seeds of division might be taken away.[6]

Basically, the first church operated on a local level with elders (also known as bishops) and deacons as the offices of the church. The offices were filled by men who had special ministerial gifts defined in Ephesians 4:11. An elder might be a pastor, or he might have the gift of evangelism. The apostle Peter called himself an elder (1 Peter 5:1), not in the sense of an older man, but in the sense of an elder who shepherds the flock. We shall look more at the office of the elder later. It appears that apostles, like Paul, Timothy, and Titus, filled a governing role but on a wider level than the local level. It might be speculated that the apostle "in the field," though not necessarily subject to the apostles and elders in Jerusalem, received recognition from them, as when Paul and Barnabas received the right hand of fellowship and were sanctioned by the Jerusalem body of elders (Acts 15, Galatians 2:9). There is no evidence that the apostles and elders at Jerusalem assumed any authoritative role of the local churches that were at a distance from Jerusalem other than pronouncements for doctrinal guidance as at the Acts 15 conference. The Jerusalem church represented the foundation of the church and had no prelate that assumed sole authority either in Jerusalem or elsewhere. It was understood that all authority was vested in Jesus Christ alone.

This principle is best understood if we recognize the principle of ministerial gifts described in Paul's letter to the Ephesian church. I believe that the major hindrance to God's ministry today is not sin, as grievous as this may be, but the lack of ministry operating as a "spiritual gift." It is not hard to see how the ministry has become a vocation, occupation, or profession. The earliest colleges in America

---

[6.] John Eadie, *The Ecclesiastical Cyclopaedia, 5th Edition* (London, UK: Charles Griffin and Company, 1875), 512.

were primarily religious schools whose first and foremost mission was to prepare candidates for service in the ministry or the community. One of the oldest professions known to mankind is that of priest or cleric. It is not that God did not intend for there to be such a vocation, but the duty of the Old Testament priest was usually fulfilled in the religious roles of ceremony. The New Testament brought about a different kind of ministry.

In reality, what has happed today is that the new wine has been poured into old bottles. This is true for the ceremony of the church. It is also true for the religious trappings, from the styles of worship to the ministerial offices. And in spite of how the "conservative" Christians might want to distance themselves from the "liberal" Christians, there are a lot of carryovers that only say that Christianity is a mingled and mixed multitude that still does not listen well to the Savior, who leads us.

Before we begin our discussion of the ministries, allow me to discuss the crisis that exists in the church today. Although not seen by most ministers in evangelical churches as a crisis, the truth is that we have lost the power of the apostolic ministry. The ministerial gifts listed in Ephesians 4:11 do not operate according to God's plan. There is a high incidence of failure among preachers and teachers of the gospel, and for the most part, the lack of true apostolic ministry only contributes to the worldly, powerless, and backslidden condition of the church today.

CHAPTER 2

So You Want to Be a Preacher

It was in 1972 that Jesus Christ saved me in a Pentecostal church in Baytown, Texas. I was water baptized in the name of Jesus Christ and received the Holy Spirit in a revival preached by an anointed young evangelist. During a prayer vigil of several days at the church, God called me to preach and gave me a vision of preaching before thousands of people. Certainly, many in ministry receive God's call in sundry ways, but prudence and experience teach us that "whom God calls, he qualifies." It is called discipleship, and while there may be exceptions, God normally does not turn out ninety-day wonders in the ministry. The Lord's example of discipleship, in which he trained his disciples for more than three years, and admonitions by Paul concerning "lay hands suddenly on no man" (1 Timothy 5:22), as well as other scriptures, suggest that there is a process by which God develops and establishes ministry and leadership within the church.

I was blessed to be under the teaching and preaching of some of the finest pastors and teachers in the Apostolic and Pentecostal movements. These men were tremendous ministers and had one thing in common: all were leaders among men, great administrators as well as great ministers. However, as we recognize the need for discipleship and mentoring as necessary for ministry to develop, we must also realize that it is through such discipleship that the influences or teaching of others will impact our own understanding of ministry, for better or worse.

It was at Texas Bible College in Houston, Texas, that God began opening doors for my own ministry. My home church of Irvington Pentecostal Church was pastored by a highly respected pastor, teacher, and presbyter, Corliss Dees. My ministry did not begin in the pulpit, except that I was able to preach some youth services. Pastor Dees had me preaching in nursing homes, working in bus ministry, and being involved in Sunday school. On one occasion, I felt a desire to step out in the field of evangelism as a traveling minister, and because Pastor Dees was well-known throughout the church organization, I asked him, "Brother Dees, could you call some of your preacher friends and give me recommendations to go preach for them?"

He answered, "No. If the Lord has called you to preach, he will open the doors for you." I was a bit offended, but I believed wholeheartedly in being submissive to the pastor and reluctantly accepted it as wisdom that I needed in my life. The answer by Pastor Dees was all about timing.

I got married while in Bible college, and during that time, God had opened doors of ministry, but the desire to step out in faith and become a traveling evangelist was spurred by the consuming fire "shut up in my bones," as it was with the prophet Jeremiah. The desire was so strong that eventually I dropped out of Bible school and quit my job at a law firm where I worked. My wife and I packed two suitcases, and off we went—by faith—with only a couple of promises of places to preach. In hindsight, I would do it again because of how God led our steps. The admonition from Pastor Dees—that if God called me to preach, he would open the doors—was indeed true. I will not give an account of those many months as an evangelist except to say that through miracles and the results of conversion, our ministry flourished.

Later while on the evangelistic field, I was asked to preach at an Illinois camp meeting where Pastor Dees was the camp speaker, and I was proud that he gave his voice to appoint me as a licensed minister. I felt like I had arrived, and true to the pastor's pronouncement, God did indeed open many opportunities for me to preach services in many cities. I was an evangelist—a revivalist. I felt like I "had arrived."

I had been preaching a series of revivals in Illinois, when one evening I said to my wife, "I wonder how many churches there are in New York?" Amazingly, the following day, S. R. Hanby, the district superintendent of the New York district of the United Pentecostal Church, called me on the phone. It was a total surprise, but it was more than coincidental considering the statement I had made the night before.

"Brother Davis," he said, "the Lord spoke to me and told me to call you. In Ithaca, New York, the district has purchased a building for a mission work. There is no congregation, and very little money, but God told me to find you and ask you to come to New York to start a mission church in Ithaca. I have called all over the country looking for you to ask you to come to New York and start a church." This is the story of my Macedonian call to begin a ministry of church planting.

For more than forty-five years, I was a church planter, opening new works in New York, Rhode Island, Virginia, Pennsylvania, South Carolina, and Florida. I soon discovered that I had many weaknesses, but I also found that the Lord could do great work even with my weaknesses and failures. I also discovered that I had this constant desire to do things my own way, believing of course that I was doing them God's way. I was able to lead. I was able to build. I was able to organize and direct, to supervise, administer. I could do many of the things that I had seen other—some more successful—ministers and pastors do so effectively. During this time, I experienced what I know most pastors experience: the usual testing of trials, temptations, and questions that come as we realize all pastors are human. Pastors not only make mistakes, but their opinions, beliefs, and character are not always aligned with God's Word. Sin, ethical lapses, and making bad decisions plague the ministry for we are just as human as all those to whom we preach.

While there are plenty of failures in the ministry, sins in the ministry usually result in consequences that either destroy a minister or become a lesson learned that results in repentance and restoration. However, not all damaging human behavior is a result of overt dis-obedience to some command of God. I mentioned bad decision making, but there can also be plenty of damage done by ignorance, lack of wisdom, character or personality flaws, and failure to "rightly divide the word of truth" (2 Timothy 2:15).

Beyond the obvious implication that false teaching does have eternal consequences, holding to the wrong understanding about something does not necessarily mean that sin is the problem and that hellfire will result for one's wrongheadedness. When Paul speaks in Romans chapter 14 about someone choosing to eat vegetables instead of meat, holding such a view does not condemn a person. However, the damage of a preacher turning the issue into a stumbling block may or may not result in eternal consequences, but the danger is that the continual ignorance of a preacher espousing "doubtful disputations" means that there is a likelihood that some hearer will go astray and fall. Then such wrongheadedness becomes a matter of judgment.

I could name a litany of damaging behavior that may not rise to the level of sin but have consequences that cause damage to the hearer in such a way as to become a stumbling block. Consider the damaging impact of preaching the truth in such an offensive manner that wounds the hearer that it makes it more difficult for the hearer to believe the gospel. Also, could holding a standard or view and preaching it in such a way that it brings condemnation to the hearer be an offense that God will judge? Note that I did not say "conviction" but "condemnation." What kind of damage is done by the temperamental slip of a pastor who "beats the sheep" during times of frustration? In short, there are plenty of things that pastors can do that might not rise to the level of sin—or will they? After all, "you must give an account on judgment day for every idle word you speak" (Matthew 12:36).

What then is the most likely failure of preachers who in sincerity strive to preach truth to others? It isn't overt sin, for although this can be a problem, it is not the biggest problem. Most preachers, I believe, sincerely try to put away sin, and they just as sincerely believe what they are preaching. However, the biggest problem in today's ministry is the damage done by willful ignorance and holding to traditions that do not align with God's Word.

The Preacher's Worldview

While in Bible college, our college president, E. L. Holley, once stated, "As a preacher, I would not stoop to be a king." He meant that there is no greater form of influence or role or vocation that can be placed on a man than that of a spokesman for God. The influence of an earthly king may extend beyond the king's lifetime but will eventually fade away. The preacher's influence has eternal significance far beyond this mortal life. It has been said, "Lawyers' mistakes are in jail, doctors' mistakes are in the grave, and preachers' mistakes are in hell." As an oracle of truth, their pronouncements are most often a matter of eternal life or death, which of all else matters the most for our existence.

It is incumbent on the oracle of truth, in this case a Christian preacher, to speak on behalf of God, the source of all truth. The preacher's philosophy and worldview must be explicitly aligned with God's worldview, for the preacher should be speaking not for the self but for God. I suggest to you that in reality, most preachers speak not for God but for themselves. Doctrinal teaching is always biased toward a theological viewpoint, and while that is expected, it is only appropriate if the theological position is truth and aligns with the Word of God, as meant by God, the author.

Much religious oratory is often tainted by lack of truth, agendas of the speakers, or misinformation, even when done with the utmost sincerity. It is contingent on preachers to continuously be immersed in self-critique, God's critique, and the critique of peers as checks and balances on maintaining complete truth. The problem is that such scrutiny by God, peers, and the Holy Spirit depends on complete honesty and humility by the ministry, who most often operate in independence and autonomy. Many of those in ministry are guilty of "mishandling" the Word of God; otherwise the "broad way" for Christianity would not exist (Matthew 7:13–14, KJV). We are reminded by scripture:

> Preach the word; be instant in season, out of season; reprove, rebuke, exhort with all long-suffer-

ing and doctrine. For the time will come when they will not endure sound doctrine; but after their own lusts shall they heap to themselves teachers, having itching ears; And they shall turn away their ears from the truth, and shall be turned unto fables. (2 Timothy 4:2–4, KJV)

So guard yourselves and God's people. Feed and shepherd God's flock—his church, purchased with his own blood—over which the Holy Spirit has appointed you as elders. I know that false teachers, like vicious wolves, will come in among you after I leave, not sparing the flock. Even some men from your own group will rise up and distort the truth in order to draw a following. (Acts 20:28–30, KJV)

Now I beseech you, brethren, mark them which cause divisions and offenses contrary to the doctrine which ye have learned; and avoid them. For they that are such serve not our Lord Jesus Christ, but their own belly; and by good words and fair speeches deceive the hearts of the simple. (Romans 16:17–18)

I marvel that ye are so soon removed from him that called you into the grace of Christ unto another gospel: Which is not another; but there be some that trouble you and would pervert the gospel of Christ. (Galatians 1:6–7)

The man that speaks for God must have God's Word in mind and heart, for "out of the abundance of the heart, the mouth speaketh" (Luke 6:45). Sadly, preaching today is not always rooted in God's Word, nor does it proceed from God's mouth—rather, from the mouth and mind of the speaker. The prophets and teachers (Acts 13:1) who were the mainstays of ministry in the early church are often replaced today by the philosophers or even entertainers who abound in all venues, religious and secular. As in Greece and Rome, the orators ascended as the oracles became extinct.

This highlights the biggest danger for any preacher: *the innate nature of self-involvement in the message.* The philosophy, the worldview, the delivery, and the results are most often intertwined with the personal motives or agendas of the preacher. In this respect, preachers can be among the most dangerous of men. While the eternal soul that belongs to God is in the hands of one who "stands in the gap" before God, the preacher that allows personal agendas to guide the preaching is more dangerous than any politician that leads a nation or any educator that leads a classroom. Consequences are eternal rather than temporal.

The only remedy is to become Christ-minded in ministry, which includes two very important characteristics of Jesus. One of these characteristics is reflected in the principle role of servant. In this role, Jesus was known as the "Son of man" who saw himself as a servant. This will be discussed further as we discuss servant-leaders and inverted authority. The second characteristic is that Jesus's ministry was not about himself or of his own will. The total submissiveness that allowed him to go to the cross was reflected in his life and was a part of his mental makeup. Both his thinking and speaking were subjugated to the mind, will, and Words of God. Subjugation means to bring under domination or under the control of another—to become subordinate.

> Jesus answered them, and said, My doctrine is not mine, but his that sent me. If any man will do his will, he shall know of the doctrine, whether it be of God, or whether I speak of myself. He that speaketh of himself seeketh his own glory: but he that seeketh his glory that sent him, the same is true, and no unrighteousness is in him. (John 7:16–18)

Preachers must not preach their own doctrine, which includes their own philosophy or worldview. If the preacher believes and holds the same doctrine, philosophy, or worldview as God, the glory and credit must be given to God. The ministry must not let personal glory become a corrupting influence on preaching. Unfortunately, the increasing elevation of the pastoral ministry is a concern and the focus of what I now call the *pastoral supremacy syndrome.*

Pastoral Supremacy

I am not sure how many God-called ministers are spoken to by God, who says, "You are going to be a pastor," or perhaps, "Your role will be that of a teacher, sitting on the pew, preaching once in a while, and never receiving a part of the tithes." There are testimonies of men and women who have received "the call" as God speaks in the spirit and lets them know that someday they will "pastor a church" or perhaps "be a missionary to Ethiopia" or some other foreign shore. The calling of missionary is the equivalent of "apostle," but chances are the word *apostle* does not come through in the moment of calling—although it might. For me, I was simply told, "You will preach before thousands of people." This was my calling in a six-night prayer vigil when I was a new convert, although there was a time of preparation, which is as it should be. It wasn't an audible voice like I heard when God called me to salvation, but then that is another story.

Paul, on the other hand, says in both Romans and Corinthians that he was "called to be an apostle" (Romans 1:1; 1 Corinthians 1:1, 15:9). He also uses the words "chosen to be apostle," but when did such a calling take place? The Acts 9 account of Paul's conversion tells us the Lord did not tell him anything about how to be an apostle or how to pastor, or even evangelize. Paul did not get the benefit of the three-year discipleship training afforded to other apostles. When the Lord spoke to Ananias, it was said of Paul, "for he is a chosen vessel unto me, to bear my name before the Gentiles, and kings, and the children of Israel" (Acts 9:15). Paul, like most God-called ministers, received on-the-job, pray-as-you-go training.

The Bible tells us that there were twelve disciples of Jesus whom he called apostles, and this designation appeared to be purposeful and in contrast with the other disciples, of which there were many. Mark writes, "And he called them his apostles" (Mark 3:14), while Luke says, "Whom also he named apostles" (Luke 6:13). The word *apostle*, from the Greek *apostolos*, simply means "messenger," but did that mean the seventy disciples that were sent forth to preach were not messengers? It is interesting to note that the word *preach* (Greek *kerysso*) was not used with the sending of the seventy, while it is used with the sending of the twelve (compare Luke 10:1–17 with Matthew 10:4–14), even though the instructions are very similar for both groups. However, *kerysso* is used in what has commonly been called the Great Commission (Matthew 28:18–20, Mark 16:15, Luke 24:47), which is generally suggested to be for all of Jesus's disciples, even though it appears that it was spoken only to the eleven.

There arises this question: are there differences between the twelve apostles and the seventy disciples that Jesus sent out to minister? While the twelve and the seventy were sent to preach the gospel, what is obvious is that the twelve apostles were set apart in their ministry from the other disciples. While functionally there are similarities between the disciples that preached and the apostles that preached, there was an intended distinction made by the given designation of "apostle." Wherever a designated term of distinction is used, a proper exegesis must be applied to understand the meaning. Words such as *elder, deacon, bishop, apostle, prophet, evangelist, pastor,* or *teacher* each has a distinctive meaning. It is obvious the term *apostle* was intended to be distinctly used for the twelve, but not for the other seventy disciples. We also know that there would be more apostles called to this distinctive ministry. In fact, the ministry of apostles would become but one of five distinctive gifts given to the church. The word *pastor* is distinct, so what does it mean and to whom should it apply? The word *evangelist* is distinct, and to whom should it apply? What are the differences in ministry? What are the differences in leadership? Did God intend for a change in usage so that in our modern era, we only have two kinds of preachers—pastors and evangelists?

The reason for getting the correct meaning for the several terms is important, because there are distinctions of function between the leadership role and the preaching role. Leadership roles are divided into two separate offices, elders and deacons; and preaching roles are divided into five separate gifts: apostle, prophet, evangelist, pastor, and teacher. Does it matter, or is this simply an exercise in semantics? The easiest way to answer is to appeal to a very simple bit of logic; everything God says and does matters in the purposes of God. Otherwise, we could just safely assume that one person who is both pastor and elder would be all that is needed in the church today. I submit, there are both preachers and saints who believe just that.

One reason for this discussion is to show how that meaning has been lost over time by cultural changes within the church, but along with the loss in meaning, structural changes in the church have made both ministry and leadership much different than the original biblical model. Some may suggest, "The changes are good because look at all the great mega churches, as well as the thousands of other churches." The truth is that all is not well. There are many abuses that are being covered up or ignored. It is not uncommon to hear of failures in the ministry, of excessive living, of immorality, or of unethical practices. Could a nonbiblical approach to church leadership be partly to blame for much of the carnality and worldliness that exist in Christianity today? If so, can we discover if there is a biblical plan for leadership that was instituted by Jesus to prevent or remedy leadership quandaries?

This book is not a conjecture on what lies in the heart of every pastor, but rather it tries to understand the reason for the troubling rise in what I have identified as pastoral supremacy syndrome, which has many symptoms. The pastoral supremacy syndrome is akin to the business world's founder's syndrome. Both syndromes are discussed in the following chapters.

The result of the pastoral supremacy syndrome is the demise of God's intended fivefold ministerial gifts and the changed nature of biblical church government. The first edition of *Restoring the Fivefold Ministry* was intended to clearly delineate the ministerial gifts of

Ephesians 4:11, known as a fivefold ministry, with the offices of church government, that of elders and deacons.

This second edition of *Restoring* expands the scope of the discussion. Because of the high level of ridicule and negativity received from many pastors after the release of the original book, this second edition adds more depth and research concerning church government models, also known as church polity. I want to note that all current models of church government can be workable where leaders and followers agree to the terms, but what matters is the biblical plan for church government based on the reasons evidenced in scripture. In addition to understanding what God's intentions are in giving ministerial gifts to the church, it is important to compare the differing view of church government with scripture to find God's intentions for the original form. The outcome of church government should be the fostering of righteousness, truth, and full submission to God, thus fulfilling the purposes of God. Structures that interject influences not rooted in truth and submission to God result in consequences that bring harm to individuals and organizations.

Truth is the fabric that creates sustainability. Lies, while powerful enough to change the course of men, eventually are destined to fail and destroy whatever they touch. It is reported that Cicero said, "Men prefer to believe what they prefer to be true," but falsehood destroys relationships, which are the basis of any society. No social structure—whether it is a church, family, business, or government—can stand when it is divided, and deception by its nature is divisive. The temporary unity of everyone believing the same lie will ultimately be shattered as the power of truth is revealed. Truth will always win out in the end, just as light dispels darkness.

The first edition of *Restoring the Fivefold Ministry* is not about preaching but about leadership and expounding on the differences between being a preacher and a church leader, and it created a plethora of negative rebuttals by many pastors and preachers who believe that only one preacher (nominally the pastor) can be the leader of the flock. On message boards both in public and private, I was ridiculed for insisting that a church can have more than one pastor. What is misunderstood is that while I believe that small churches may function well with one pastor, it is not God's intended model for church government. Moreover, this book endeavors to show that holding to such an idea not only disregards Bible truth but results in the unintended consequence of faulty leadership that will result in preaching falsehoods. I contend that any preacher that preaches the supremacy of the pastor (now a common problem) is contributing to a fallacy that is responsible for the overall demise of God's plan in Ephesians 4, wherein ministerial gifts are plainly set forth. The supremacy of the pastor mantra is fraught with abuses that result in what I call the *Peter, Paul, Apollos syndrome* of 1 Corinthians1:10–13. It is often the cause of church splits, discouraged workers, inappropriate pastoral conduct, and ethical lapses within the ministry.

An oracle of truth is essential for the church, but it is unsound to believe that one oracle is safe. Paul wrote, "In the mouth of two or three witnesses shall every word be established" (2 Corinthians 13:1). It may be that within a local church there is a primary preacher, but instead of pastor, the primary preacher might be an evangelist, an apostle, a prophet, or a teacher. What must be understood is that preachers (referring to the fivefold ministry) and leaders (referring to elders and deacons) are distinct and different roles. The role of elder is static, meaning that there are qualifications and required structural elements. The role of preacher, however, is dynamic, meaning that there are different styles of ministry and purpose; preachers are gifted in one of the ministerial gifts or may change in ministerial gift and purpose.

One person may function within both roles simultaneously, but to assume that there can only be one sole pastor—and one sole elder—who occupies exclusive sole authority in the church is in stark contrast to the Lord's meaning when Jesus said, "Ye know that they which are accounted to rule over the Gentiles exercise lordship over them; and their great one exercise authority upon them. But so shall it not be among you" (Mark 10:42–43). Often an unintended consequence of a single-pastor church is that of replacing the lordship of Christ with the lordship of the pastor. The institution of a biblical church structure of collegial elders and deacons functioned to provide checks and balances to the individual control of one person in leadership. The two major theses for *Restoring* is that God intended collegial eldership (more than one person sharing authority) for the leadership of the church, and that the term *pastor*, as well as those of the other Ephesian 4:11 gifts, is just that—preaching gifts delineated by style and purpose.

Today's common perception for church leadership is that of a person who is both preacher and pastor, while biblically, neither may be the case. A preacher in a local church may not be a pastor at all as to gift, and it is possible that some of the elders in a local church may not be preaching elders. All elders function in a pastoral role, and as such, elder and pastor can be used synonymously. However, the issue is understanding the pastoral gift in the context of the fivefold ministry, but also understanding the elder's office. The preaching elder might be an evangelist or an apostle, both of which differ from the ministerial gift of pastor. Somehow it is this fact that is lost upon the church who calls the main preaching elder *pastor* and that has "pastoral appreciation days," which demeans others of the fivefold ministry who languish on the pew.

Consider the very important scriptural text that ties the concept of preacher remuneration with the concept of leadership in the church:

> Let the elders that rule well be counted worthy of double honor, especially they who labor in the word and doctrine. For the scripture saith, Thou shall not muzzle the ox that treadeth out the corn, and the laborer is worthy of his reward. (1 Timothy 5:17–18, 20)

The scripture is speaking of the financial support of church leaders, who in the above context are referred to as elders, who are more than one in number, and whose job is to "rule" (not specifically that of preaching), but with the caveat that those elders who also preach are worthy of double honor. The implication by the caveat is that there are elders who do not preach but rule. Church leadership is not solely vested in a "preacher," although being "apt to teach" is one of the requirements for the leadership role in the church. Nor is the tithing that is most often associated with the preacher limited to preaching elders, although such preachers deserve greater remuneration. The pastoral term is used in a broad sense because the church is metaphorically "the flock," but the specific term *pastor* is used but once in the New Testament (Ephesians 4:11) and as such should be viewed in the context of the scripture in which it is included.

This book is a compendium to *Restoring the Fivefold Ministry.*[7] While some of the original work is incorporated into the second edition, the intent is to help, not destroy, the concept of pastoral leadership by putting it in its rightful place as one of the ministerial gifts. The true biblical concept of multiple elders conjointly leading a flock is well-documented in scripture, and only the stubbornness of a Diotrephes, "who loveth to have the preeminence" (1 John 1:9), could cause today's pastor to not want God's original plan for the church. Church leadership is first and foremost about being a servant leader, and if that also entails being a preacher, we must renounce the hidden things of dishonesty, "not walking in craftiness, nor handling the word of God deceitfully" (2 Corinthians 4:2).

There are several concepts that shall be added to the original treatise of *Restoring*. These include a discussion on founder's syndrome, which is common in business and in the church. Second, I shall expose in more detail the roots of the Peter, Paul, Apollos syndrome—that is, the problem with preacher religion, which is evident in our modern church. This is sometimes evidenced by excesses in the world of televangelists and sustained by such practices as pastoral appreciation days and other symbols of pastoral supremacy syndrome, which contribute to the misunderstanding of the biblical teaching of fivefold ministry. I will also write on servant leadership, which has roots in the Lord's pronouncement to his disciples about authority in the church (Mark 10:35–45).

[7.] Paul Davis, *Restoring the Fivefold Ministry* (Coral Springs, FL: Llumina Press, 2004).

CHAPTER 3

The First Mega Church

"And when the day of Pentecost was fully come, they were all with one accord in one place. And suddenly there came a sound from heaven as of a rushing mighty wind, and it filled all the house where they were sitting. And there appeared unto them cloven tongues like as of fire, and it sat upon each of them. And they were all filled with the Holy Ghost, and began to speak with other tongues, as the Spirit gave them utterance" (Acts 2:1–4, KJV).

A preacher once quipped that the biggest miracle on the day of Pentecost wasn't the speaking in tongues, nor was it even the fact they were all in one accord. The biggest miracle, he said, was that they were all in one place. This alludes, of course, to the problem in churches of having all the folks turn out for service. In reality, the great miracle that day was indeed the outpouring of the Holy Spirit, which endued the disciples with power to become witnesses throughout the world. While the gifts of the Ephesians 4 ministry are a distinct set of gifts, the inherent gift of being a witness, the anointing to speak the gospel to all men, is a universal gift. The anointing of the Holy Spirit distributes many gifts, and all of them are intended as gifts of service to the church and to the purpose of God in establishing his kingdom throughout the world.

The word *church* from the Greek *ekklesia* refers variably to a calling out, a popular meeting, or an assembly called for a purpose. While Christians also have a broader definition, meaning the whole body of Christ, the literal reference to the local assembly is the basic New Testament meaning applied to the many groups that sprang up in places like Jerusalem, Ephesus, Rome, or Corinth. It is likely that the local churches ranged in size from small to large, and there is biblical evidence that most met in homes, although it is also likely that as they grew, they adopted meeting places similar to the synagogue style of meeting already common among the Jews. One example is in Corinth, where the church moved into the school of Tyrannus (Acts 19:9).

A few days prior to Pentecost, there were 120 disciples of Jesus Christ who met to watch and pray for the fulfillment of the Holy Spirit prophecy according to the Lord's instructions. The *church* of 120 "continued with one accord in prayer and supplication, with the women, and Mary the mother of Jesus, and with his brethren" (Acts 1:4). These prayer meetings took place in an upper room, and it was during that time that a replacement for Judas was chosen to be numbered with the other eleven original apostles who had been chosen by Jesus Christ to be the first world missionaries. An understanding of the ministry of apostles as missionary is helped when we understand that the Great Commission as recorded in Matthew 28:16–20 and Mark 16:14–18 was given directly to the eleven rather than the church as a whole.

When the day of Pentecost came, the church had moved from the upper room to the temple because of the customary pilgrimage surrounding the feast of Pentecost. It was at the temple that the promised Holy Spirit, accompanied by the miracle of speaking in tongues, descended upon the disciples of Jesus Christ. The Bible declares, "And they were all filled with the Holy Ghost, and began to speak with other tongues, as the Spirit gave them utterance" (Acts 2:4). All those that heard the speaking in tongues were Jews of the pilgrimage, but they lived in foreign lands, including Jews from Mesopotamia, Judaea, Cappadocia, Asia, Egypt, Libya, Rome, and elsewhere. There were also proselytes, or Gentiles who had converted to Judaism. Some theologians contend that speaking in tongues was used in order for the listeners to be able to understand what was preached—that is, "missionary tongue." However, these were Jewish people who were Hebrew speakers, although bilingual according to the nation in which they lived. When Peter later addressed the crowd, he spoke to them in one language, the Hebrew language, which needed no interpretation. Peter did not preach to them in tongues.

The result of this great miracle was the preaching of the first gospel message to what would become Jewish believers who would afterward return to their homelands to carry the good news of Jesus and the fulfilled promise of the baptism of the Holy Spirit. Even so, while many were to return home carrying the gospel, a large number would remain in Jerusalem. There is no indication of how many of the three thousand souls "added unto them" (Acts 2:41) would remain in Jerusalem to become a part of the local church, but the beginning of the first "mega church" is quickly recorded in biblical church history. The Bible tells us, "And the Lord added to the church daily such as should be saved" (Acts 2:47), and within a short span of time, following the end of the Pentecost pilgrimage, the continued preaching, teaching, and miracles that took place in Jerusalem resulted in five thousand more men plus women being added to the number (Acts 4:4).

If we considered the impact of such a great revival in our modern era, we would be contemplating such questions as where did they meet? Did they have multiple church schedules to handle the crowds? And who was the pastor or evangelist? So often, the focus is on the personalities of the ministry rather than on the work of the Lord Jesus Christ.

CHAPTER 4

Organizational Identity

O f all the organizations in the world, the church stands out among the oldest organizational entities in existence. The beginning of the church is commonly dated from the day of Pentecost in AD 30. The Hebrew calendar shows this to be year 3790, month of Sivan, Sunday the eighth. For the Roman calendar, it would be Sunday, May 28 of AD 30.[8] Depending on how the term *organization* is applied, one source claims the Japanese monarchy has a continuous history from 660 BC, while the oldest business in recent history is said to be a temple builder in Japan, the Kongo Gumi Company, founded in AD 576.[9] However, Kongo Gumi was finally absorbed as a subsidiary of Takamutsu in 2006, ending its 1,400-year claim to being the oldest independent company in existence. Another claim to the oldest extant organization is the ShiShi High School in Chengdu, Sichuan, China, which claims heritage from the Han dynasty in 141 BC. However, even this venerable institution has been destroyed several times in its history. I submit to you that the oldest continually existing organization in the world today is the church of Jesus Christ. The reason for the claim is supported by the fact that its organizational identity and structure are such that it not only has outlasted all

8. Church of God Study Forum, "Hebrew-Roman Calendar Comparisons." Retrieved from http://www.cgsf.org/dbeattie/calendar/?roman=30.
9. "Kongo Gumi Construction," *Business Today* (November 29, 2011), https://businessestoday.wordpress.com/tag/kongo-gumi-construction/.

organizations of historical significance but has eternal sustainability. By understanding God's purpose for the church, we can understand better our own purpose for being a part of the church. In this book, we are focused primarily on the purpose of ministers, who have the great responsibility to see that God's purpose for the church is carried out. I must clearly state that the purpose of God for the church is not thousands of people sitting on the pews as religious spectators of singers and preachers; it is preaching a gospel of reconciliation to a world of sinners.

Although we can view organizational structures in various ways, the family being the oldest, for our purpose we are looking at organizations that are considered organic and that exist in the realm of business, society, or government. Whether a business or a government, organizational identity is most importantly based on its purpose and mission. Amy Adkins simplifies organizational identity as "three interrelated elements: purpose, brand, and culture."[10] The church's organizational identity includes the purpose (mission), its culture (ministry), its branding (message), and I suggest another part of its cultural identity is how it operates (methods). The cultural aspect for the church is all about its people. This includes its leaders and members and answers the following questions: how do the people in the church have relationships, how are relationships developed and maintained, and most importantly, how do the people within the organization (both leaders and members) serve the purpose of the organization? Metaphorically, the church is both a business (the "father's business" [Luke 2:49]) and a government (that is, the "kingdom of heaven") and has what is commonly termed a "social contract" with those who are subjects of its organization. Friend (n.d.) explains social contract theory as being associated with the philosophies of Hobbes, Locke, and Rousseau, who between the sixteenth and eighteenth centuries argued that there were moral and political obligations between government and subjects that serve as an agreement between the two parties of the ruler(s) and those that

---

[10.] Amy Adkins, "B2b Organic Growth Demands a Strong Organizational Identity," *Gallup Business Journal* 19 (2016): para. 7.

are ruled.[11] In the case of the church, these are the old and new covenants that have existed from the giving of the law on Mount Sinai to the present day. These are not to be confused with the individual covenants to Noah, Abraham, or Jacob, for the Old and New Testaments (or covenants) are between God and his people as a whole.

However, it is the purpose of an organization that gives life to the organization. Of all the elements that create organizational identity, purpose is the one thing that must not be lost. All else, brand and culture, must be aligned with purpose for an organization to survive. Amy Adkins observes, "Everything follows purpose. An organization's purpose, or mission, tells the world why it's here, what it stands for and—just as importantly—what it does not stand for. As the guiding principle for actions, behaviors and decisions, purpose rarely changes; rather, it evolves."[12]

The mission of the church, its purpose, has been—from the first Passover—the message of deliverance from the bondage and suffering of sin though the atoning blood of one sacrificial lamb, without spot or blemish. Reconciliation to God comes by faith, and we that have been so reconciled are responsible for propagating the good news of reconciliation throughout the world. The mission is kingdom building for Jesus Christ, who is God our Savior, King of kings, and Lord of lords. There is no greater mission, and the mission has not changed.

Familiar to most Christians is that part of scripture that has been called the Great Commission. Before his ascension, the Lord gave instructions to his eleven remaining disciples, saying,

> All power is given unto me in heaven and in earth. Go ye therefore, and teach all nations, baptizing them in the name of the Father, and of the Son, and of the Holy Ghost: Teaching them to observe all things whatsoever I have commanded

---

[11.] Celeste Friend (n.d.), "Social Contract Theory," *Internet Encyclopedia of Philosophy*. Retrieved from https://www.iep.utm.edu/soc-cont/.

[12.] Adkins, "Purpose," para. 10.

you: and, lo, I am with you always, even unto the end of the world. Amen. (Matthew 28:19–20)

Also,

And said unto them, Thus it is written, and thus it behoved Christ to suffer, and to rise from the dead the third day: And that repentance and remission of sins should be preached in his name among all nations, beginning at Jerusalem. And ye are witnesses of these things. And, behold, I send the promise of my Father upon you: but tarry ye in the city of Jerusalem, until ye be endued with power from on high. (Luke 24:46–49)

The Great Commission is understood to be the primary purpose of the church and answers the questions of *what the purpose of the church is, how is it to be carried out,* and *who are the people involved.* While specifically given to the disciples that were chosen to be the first apostles, it is understood that by their teaching others "to observe all things whatsover I have commanded you," it meant that as they were discipled by Jesus Christ, they were to disciple others in the same manner. Whatever commands were given to them were to be given to all that were discipled, including the fact that they were to disciple others who would, in turn, disciple others.

What should be seen from the Great Commission is that the Lord intended not a church made up of spectators but one made up of disciples who serve the purposes of God through the mission of the church. Discipleship begins with leadership that has been equipped with five different gifts that are given to the church to equip the saints to fulfill God's purpose. Apostle Paul writes,

And he gave some, apostles; and some, prophets; and some, evangelists; and some, pastors and teachers; For the perfecting of the saints, for the work of the ministry, for the edifying of the body

35

of Christ: Till we all come in the unity of the
faith, and of the knowledge of the Son of God,
unto a perfect man, unto the measure of the stature of the fullness of Christ. (Ephesians 4:11–13)

Sadly it is apparent that the ministry of the fivefold gifts does
not go on in many churches that depend entirely on a good music
ministry and a good preacher to draw the crowds that feed the semblance of what is supposed to be the church of Jesus Christ. God's
church does exist, and it does function, but so many sincere and
honest ministries come short of God's full purpose, and many church
members also fail in fulfilling the purpose of God for their own lives.
In the latter case, sadly it is poor leadership that contributes to the
hindrances that create that lack of fulfillment.

The Mission of the Church

What characteristics would satisfy the strictest definition for
oldest continual organization in existence? While some religions may
claim to precede the Christian religion, the church should be seen to
include the whole Judeo-Christian faith, which is organized around
the specific worship of the One True God, has a body of laws and
literature that are tied together, and include both the Jewish faith and
the Christian faith. While there is some reason to acknowledge that
true worshipers go back to the beginning of human history, the organized church should consider the first exodus of Israel from bondage
in Egypt—and the first Passover as a marker for a first unified religious expression of faith, a ceremony, which defines the primary purpose and mission of the church. The primary purpose for the church,
both under the old covenant and the new covenant, is to propagate
the good news that man can be reconciled with God through the
atoning blood of a sacrificial lamb, and that this reconciliation provides deliverance from the bondage of sin and suffering at the hands
of whatever agent opposes God and his relationship with his people.
Don Roth writes that the date of the first Passover, according to bibli-

cal calendar reckoning, is the fourteenth day of Nisan (around April), either in the year 2450 or 2666 Anno Mundi in Egypt. Anno Mundi is the calendar designation "from the year of creation," but different dates are assumed in biblical chronology depending on usage of the Byzantine calendar or the Hebrew calendar, both of which are considered for biblical dating.

In contrast to nations and governments, the church has outlasted and survived all possible wars against the kingdom of God, while nation after nation throughout history has fallen. The prophet Daniel outlined a history of major governments, such as Babylon, the Medo-Persian Empire, the Grecian Empire, and the Roman Empire, all of which no longer exist in the same form as at the height of their power (Daniel 7 and 8). While nations exist that were a part of these former empires, the empires themselves have long since fallen and cannot claim to be having a continual existence. Most evident is their change in power structure, the change in boundaries, the change in leadership, and their change in global influence. Contrast these great nations with the church, which has extended its reach throughout the world, still has the same leader, its power and influence remain the same, and the purpose remains the same.

What then is this organizational entity that is known as *the church*? There are fractured expressions, often called denominations, and the Judeo part of the church and the Christian part of the church are most often seen in separation, with a modified bridge that labels itself as "messianic." From God's point of view, however, the church includes all worshipers of the One True God from the beginning of creation. It is foolish to separate Old and New Testament writings, so the term *Holy Bible* as the written expressions of the Word of God must include both and should not be seen independent of one another. The Judeo-Christian faith represents the whole of the church and is often perceived to be two different religions, but the reality is that the biblical concept for the church is one God who is worshiped by both Jews and Gentiles, sharing the common purpose of reconciling sinful man to God through blood atonement. While the adherents of the Jewish faith and the Christian faith often forget that we are not two peoples, God's holy Word declares that we are but one based on the following text:

> This is the church of the living God, which is the pillar and foundation of the truth. (1 Timothy 3:15)

> But ye are come unto mount Sion, and unto the city of the living God, the heavenly Jerusalem, and to an innumerable company of angels, To the general assembly and church of the first-born, which are written in heaven, and to God the Judge of all, and to the spirits of just men made perfect, And to Jesus the mediator of the new covenant, and to the blood of sprinkling, that speaketh better things than that of Abel. (Hebrews 12:22–23)

> For this cause I bow my knees unto the Father of our Lord Jesus Christ, Of whom the whole family in heaven and earth is named. (Ephesians 3:14–15)

> Wherefore remember, that ye being in time past Gentiles in the flesh, who are called Uncircumcision by that which is called the Circumcision in the flesh made by hands; That at that time ye were without Christ, being aliens from the commonwealth of Israel, and strangers from the covenants of promise, having no hope, and without God in the world: But now in Christ Jesus ye who sometimes were far off are made nigh by the blood of Christ.

> For he is our peace, who hath made both one, and hath broken down the middle wall of par-

tition between us; Having abolished in his flesh the enmity, even the law of commandments contained in ordinances; for to make in himself of twain one new man, so making peace; And that he might reconcile both unto God in one body by the cross, having slain the enmity thereby: And came and preached peace to you which were afar off, and to them that were nigh. For through him we both have access by one Spirit unto the Father.

Now therefore ye are no more strangers and foreigners, but fellow citizens with the saints, and of the household of God; And are built upon the foundation of the apostles and prophets, Jesus Christ himself being the chief corner stone; In whom all the building fitly framed together groweth unto an holy temple in the Lord: In whom ye also are builded together for an habitation of God through the Spirit. (Ephesians 2:11–22, KJV)

Before the Passover, the people of God included Abraham, Isaac, Jacob, and many others as far back as Adam, Abel, or Seth. After the Exodus, and in the wilderness, the expressions of faith and worship became more formalized, and the people of God became known by a multitude of names, such as "the congregation," "the saints," "my people," and "the church," which are terms used in both the Old and New Testaments referring to the people of God. The explicit term *church* (from the Greek *ekklesia*, meaning "assembly, or those called out to a public assembly") is used in Acts 7:38, referring to the nation of Israel during the time of wilderness wanderings, but also for the specific organization to be established throughout the world following the death of Jesus Christ (Matthew 16:18, KJV). In both cases, the Jewish faith and the Christian faith became formalized and are joined together by the common purpose of worshiping the One

True God and propagating God's plan for salvation from sin. It is not unrealistic, therefore, to date the formal organization beginning from the first Passover, since this is its first formal pronouncement of purpose.

Perhaps the finest distinctive identity for the church as an organization can be summed up in the words of the apostle Peter, who wrote,

> But ye are a chosen generation, a royal priesthood, an holy nation, a peculiar people; that ye should shew forth the praises of him who hath called you out of darkness into his marvelous light: Which in time past were not a people, but are now the people of God: which had not obtained mercy, but now have obtained mercy. (1 Peter 2:9–10, KJV)

With these things in mind, we can understand that the church as an organization, and as possibly the oldest organization in existence, can make the claim that its organizational structure, its purpose, its branding (message), and its culture lend themselves to the organizational identity of a global church, the kingdom of God on earth today. Each element of organizational identity is a pillar of strength, and we as the church must know and understand the values that are inherent in the mission, ministry, message, and methods that have been given us through the foundation of the prophets and apostles of the church (Luke 11:49, Ephesians 2:20, Ephesians 3:5, 2 Peter 3:2).

The Message of the Church

While the message (gospel) of the church is the product and brand, the modern church unfortunately has adopted many messages, creating a new form of commercialization that now means the organizational growth of the church depends on the shopping habits of those who would become part of the church. Because the gospel of Jesus Christ represents the primary brand for the church, those who preach the gospel (death, burial, and resurrection of Jesus Christ) and those who obey the gospel are a part of the organization. However, like any organization, bad actors exist within. On the one hand, it would seem that the many factions within Christianity represent multiple churches, and perhaps some believe that the God of the Methodist is not the God of the Baptist, but Jesus Christ has only one church. Within the church there exist both true and false elements. The church includes those that are true to serving God and those that serve themselves. Paul writes,

> Now I beseech you, brethren, mark them which cause divisions and offenses contrary to the doctrine which ye have learned; and avoid them. For they that are such serve not our Lord Jesus Christ, but their own belly; and by good words and fair speeches deceive the hearts of the simple. (Romans 16:17–18, KJV)

> Brethren be followers together of me and mark them which walk so as ye have us for an ensample [sic example]. (For many walk of whom I have told you often, and now tell you even weeping, that they are the enemies of the cross of Christ: Whose end is destruction, whose God is their belly, and whose glory is in their shame, who mind earthly things. (Philippians 3:17–19)

The purpose (or message), even when preached in truth, can be preached with the wrong motives. It does not mean the message is wrong; it means the messenger is wrong. Consider that Paul acknowledged that even truth can be preached by false prophets. He writes,

> Some indeed preach Christ even of envy and strife; and some also of good will: The one preach Christ of contention, not sincerely, supposing

> to add affliction to my bonds: But the other of love, knowing that I am set for the defense of the gospel. What then? notwithstanding, every way, whether in pretense, or in truth, Christ is preached; and I therein do rejoice, yea, and will rejoice. (Philippians 1:15–18)

The above scriptures are referring to falsehood not outside of the church but inside the church. The Bible refers to false apostles (2 Corinthians 11:13), false teachers (2 Peter 2:1, Matthew 7:15), and false shepherds (Ezekiel 34). Within the church there are those who know the truth, and preach some truth, but because of self-serving reasons have used the gospel of Jesus Christ for their own purposes.

The Ministry of the Church

It is tempting to look at denominations in Christianity as different churches and categorize all others, not of our own denomination, as not being a part of the church. In the same way, it is tempting to look at preachers in those different denominations as being either false prophets or totally in error. Indeed there are some false religions and false preachers that call themselves Christian that are truly outside of the body of Christ. Paul writes,

> But I fear, lest by any means, as the serpent beguiled Eve through his subtilty, so your minds should be corrupted from the simplicity that is in Christ. For if he that cometh preacheth another Jesus, whom we have not preached, or if ye receive another spirit, which ye have not received, or another gospel, which ye have not accepted, ye might well bear with him. (2 Corinthians 11:3–4)

I will not make any judgment here, knowing that only God knows the heart. Suffice it to say those who know Jesus Christ as

God manifested in the flesh are aware that there are "false teachers" that deny "the only Lord God, and our Lord Jesus Christ" (Jude 1:4). However, the vast majority of preachers within the various Christian denominations preach the death, burial, and resurrection of Jesus Christ, which is the gospel (1 Corinthians 15:1–4) and which is the core message or purpose for the church. Preachers, in what is considered mainline Christianity, for the most part are sincere, true to their convictions, and have the same desires as others who have the same calling in their lives. However, sincerity is not salvation. For example, Ponce de Leon spent his own personal fortune and the lives of his soldiers in the quest of finding the "fountain of youth." No one should doubt his sincerity, but Ponce De Leon was sincerely wrong.

Sadly the church is fractured into many denominations, while whole denominations are fractured into smaller groups that consider themselves a separate denomination. The *World Christian Encyclopedia* database notes,

> As defined here, world Christianity consists of 6 major ecclesiastico-cultural blocs, divided into 300 major ecclesiastical traditions, composed of over 33,000 distinct denominations in 238 countries, these denominations themselves being composed of over 3,400,000 worship centers, churches or congregations."[13]

The 6 denominational blocs include 22,000 independent organizations, 9,000 Protestant denominations, 600 marginals, 781 Orthodox groups, 242 Roman Catholic groups, and 168 Anglican denominations. For example, the encyclopedia lists 322 denominations of Baptists, 300 denominations of Presbyterians, 123 denominations of Methodists, and 218 denominations of Adventists.

[13.] David B. Barrett, George T. Kurian, and Todd M. Johnson, "World Christian Encyclopedia: A Comparative Survey of Churches and Religions in the Modern World," in *World Christian Encyclopedia* (New York: Oxford University Press, 2001).

It is interesting that the above material comes from the Center for the Study of Global Christianity and includes a separate comment from the research assistant, which segregates "Oneness" apostolic churches, saying, "Someone might complain about the Oneness groups being included because they reject the Holy Trinity (one God in three distinct persons) and the historic Creeds, but that's how *Barrett's Encyclopedia* categorizes them, for whatever reason."[14] As an apostolic preacher myself, I have a Christian worldview that agrees that the gospel of Jesus Christ is preached by many in other denominations, but that the obedience to the gospel is not being preached due to a lack of understanding or even blind deception.

Here is the significance. Apollos was a preacher that was "fervent in the spirit, knowing only the baptism of John" (Acts 18:25). Would Apollos be considered a part of the church as a disciple of John? Would the twelve disciples of John at Ephesus who received the new birth of water and spirit be considered a part of the church (Acts 19:1–5)? If we understand the church to be inclusive of Old Testament and New Testament saints, the answer would be yes. But was Apollos preaching the gospel of Jesus Christ? He was preaching what John the Baptist preached, which—while true—was incomplete. What is evident is that Apollos was not preaching salvation to those he ministered to because he could not preach what he did not know; and John's message, while a message of repentance, was not the gospel message that saves. John's message, like the Law of Moses, was one that directed us to Christ. Aquila and Priscilla had to expound unto him "the way of God more perfectly" (Acts 18:26).

It is important to know the difference between truth, falsehood, and partial truth. Partial truth does not mean partial falsehood mixed with truth. Partial truth can be fully true but be incomplete. As a preacher, I can say, "Verily, verily I say unto thee, except a man be born again, he cannot see the kingdom of God." If I say nothing more, I have still told the truth, but the hearer who hears it and

---

14. Justin J. Evans, "The Facts and Stats on 33,000 Denominations" (Gordon-Corwell Theological Seminary), http://www.philvaz.com/apologetics/a106.htm.

believes it will still not be saved unless they understand and obey the full meaning. Jesus completed the message of salvation by qualifying the new birth in saying, "Verily, verily, I say unto thee, Except a man be born of water and of the Spirit, he cannot enter into the kingdom of God." Then by explaining necessary faith in Calvary, saying,

> And as Moses lifted up the serpent in the wilderness, even so must the Son of man be lifted up: That whosoever believeth in him should not perish but have eternal life. For God so loved the world, that he gave his only begotten Son, that whosoever believeth in him should not perish, but have everlasting life. (John 3:14–16, KJV)

Note that within the church, complete falsehood is seldom the case, although it does exist. The greater problem is that so often partial truth is being preached rather than complete falsehood. As ministers of the gospel, we must become like Paul, the apostle, who said,

> For I have not shunned to declare unto you all the counsel of God. Take heed therefore unto yourselves, and to all the flock, over the which the holy Ghost hath made you overseers, to feed the church of God, which He hath purchased with his own blood. (Acts 20:27–28, KJV)

CHAPTER 5

Christians on the Broadway

Let's begin with an unpleasant premise; many Christians are not going to be saved. The question is why. Is there a reason to believe such a thing? Jesus provided many warnings that such would be the case, as in the context of some of the kingdom parables. One parable is a parable of fish that were caught and then discarded. This parable was not about fish that were never caught.

> Again, the kingdom of heaven is like unto a net, that was cast into the sea, and gathered of every kind: Which, when it was full, they drew to shore, and sat down, and gathered the good into vessels, but cast the bad away.[49] So shall it be at the end of the world: the angels shall come forth and sever the wicked from among the just. (Matthew 13:47–49)

But more explicitly in the following direct statement:

> Not everyone that saith unto me, Lord, Lord, shall enter into the kingdom of heaven; but he that doeth the will of my father which is in heaven. Many will say to me in that day, Lord, Lord, have we not prophesied in thy name? and in thy name

have cast out devils? and in thy name done many wonderful works? And then will I profess unto them, I never knew you: depart from me, ye that work iniquity. (Matthew 7:21–23, KJV)

For humanity as a whole, we are told, "Because strait is the gate, and narrow is the way, which leadeth unto life, and few there be that find it" (Matthew 7:14). It is obvious the majority of the world is lost, and there should be great sadness in the heart of every preacher of the gospel for the possibility that the souls of believers should be turned away from heaven's gate—yet we know this is going to happen.

It is true, every person must work out their own salvation with fear and trembling, but this does not lessen the responsibility for those who are overseers in terms of two distinct activities: leadership and preaching. The distinction between leadership roles and preaching roles is important as we must weigh heavily the fact that the act of preaching is exclusively spiritual in nature while the role of elders and deacons requires a spiritual person to act in both a spiritual and temporal capacity. As we shall discuss later, let me point out that the "ordaining of elders" has always been done through a process involving other church leaders, while the call to ministry is exclusively to the individual to whom God gives a spiritual gift. Men ordain elders; God ordains preachers. Leadership entails activities both in and out of the pulpit, while preaching is a specific kind of event that is spiritual in nature.

Preaching, I submit, by design is of weightier consequences because of the spiritual purpose, and because there is solemnness attached to the preacher to be a spokesman of God. Preaching is not a temporal activity. The apostles understood this from the beginning when they designated the first deacons in the church, but said of themselves, "But we will give ourselves continually to prayer and to the ministry of the word" (Acts 6:4). In order for a preacher to be spiritually effective, he or she must be called by God, gifted by God, and anointed by God to speak his Word. Preachers are not ordained by men, and no organizational license or Bible college degree makes a preacher. The problem is that there is an enormous number of people that fill the pulpits, or the airwaves of radio or television, who are suspect as to their purpose, if not their calling. Let me describe some nonbiblical types, which I shall call preacher wannabes:

The Entertainer

It is not necessarily true that mega churches exist as a product of the charismatic entertaining preachers who often are most noticed as the "televangelist" of this modern age. There are lots of things that contribute to the growth of churches. But there are a great number of preachers today who are experts of marketing, entertainment, and attention getting—using all the techniques of showmanship. Sadly there are lesser known preachers filling pulpits today that are part-time "stand-up comics." This is not to disparage humor in delivery on occasion, but the question will be, does it suit the purpose of the message at hand? In general, the use of "entertainment" as a vehicle for attracting a crowd in order to deliver the gospel message is seen as "becoming all things to all men." But does the entertainment factor replace the "drawing of the spirit," the "anointing of the Holy Ghost," and the "power of the gospel" with men's devices? I believe the entertainer is often guilty of that kind of preaching, and this contributes greatly to the worldliness and carelessness that exist in the church today.

The Philosopher

Many preachers today resort to reason, rationalization, and worldly wisdom as sources for ministry. Many commentaries are sermon notes eventually put into print. Certainly the advent of the internet has opened up a wealth of material, but prior to the internet, there were the libraries of books, articles, and sermon illustrations available for use by preachers. These often became the source for the sermon rather than the Holy Bible. Having such material can greatly supplement a sermon, but there is nothing written by man that can substitute for or replace the Word of God as the basis for preaching to God's church. In addition, if the anointing of the Holy Spirit and quickening of God's Spirit in the mind and heart is not there while the sermon is being prepared or being delivered, all you have left is what I allude to here—reason, rationalization, and worldly wisdom. The apostle Paul had a lot to say about the subject in his first letter to the Corinthian church:

> Now we have received, not the spirit of the world, but the spirit which is of God; that we might know the things that are freely given to us of God. Which things also we speak, not in the words which man's wisdom teacheth, but which the Holy Ghost teacheth; comparing spiritual things with spiritual. (1 Corinthians 2:12–13)

The Psychologist

Whether it is in preaching "prosperity doctrine" or something else, "mind manipulators" abound in preaching today. It even comes to the surface at times with true ministers of the gospel, for there are times when human nature takes over and personal agendas become the stuff of the message. It is easy for most preachers to find themselves depending more and more on psychological experience than on anointing—particularly since most preachers are either additionally trained in psychology, or simply sensitive to human nature because of the presence of God's spirit in their lives. As preachers, we deal with human nature all the time. We are regularly involved in the trials and temptations of the lives of people to whom we minister. We are sometimes caseworkers, family therapists, or police officers. We try to be lawyers, judges, or doctors. We are so involved with the psychology of people that if we are not careful, we become attuned more to the human psyche than the spirit (*psyche*) of God when it comes time to do the preaching.

The Professor

I love church history, and there are times when using it is appropriate for a sermon. There are great benefits to understanding the culture, language, and idioms for Bible times and peoples. Jesus was a master in using illustrations of common and ordinary events for his parables and sermons. But teaching happens on many levels. The elementary school teacher would not give a class on the level of graduate school material to a sixth grader. However, there are some preachers who are convinced that "knowledge is salvation." There are whole church denominations that focus on reaching the intellectual part of man and show disdain to churches who show too much emotion as a part of their church norms. There certainly is a part of church society that loves the lofty, gives particular credence to the credentials of a preacher, and doesn't mind the existential when it comes to preaching. Here is a good scriptural principle to remember: "Now as touching things offered unto idols, we know that we all have knowledge. Knowledge puffeth up, but charity edifieth" (1 Corinthians 8:1).

The Imitators

We are all sponges when it comes to learning behaviors. Seldom is there a time when every word we speak in a sermon is an original thought or revelation. Timothy surely quoted Paul as he preached in Ephesus, and our sermon quotes are not only from scripture but from our pastors and teachers. It's a great honor to sit under the ministry of great men of God who have great preaching ministries. I thank the several preachers who have contributed much to my own education in ministry, and I believe their influence has come through in my own preaching. I have often rejoiced when I hear young men who have been under my ministry present those things that I have taught, making references to remarks that I have made and sometimes quoting my own words as a part of their sermon material. However, with the advent of new technology, sermon material and even whole sermons are available as never before. This creates opportunity to be a blessing or can be a problem if too much dependence exists on material that comes from these sources.

Salvation Is a Process

I am unapologetically a "One God, baptized in Jesus's name, Holy Spirit filled, tongue talking" Christian. I often tag my church advertising and websites with the tagline, "Apostolic in Doctrine and Pentecostal in Experience." Some call those of our faith "Jesus Only," others speak of us as "Oneness," but as many of us apostolic preachers do, I tell people, "I'm not Jesus only. I'm Jesus everything." Hopefully there are plenty of non-Oneness Christians reading this book so that you will understand that many apostolic preachers do not discredit the work of Jesus Christ in the lives of believers in other denominations. Someone once said to a Oneness preacher, "Brother, you must believe that only you apostolics are going to heaven." To which the apostolic preacher replied, "No, brother, that's not what I believe. I don't believe that even all of us are going." However, those of us in ministry should remember that we are not the judges. Again I am reminded of Apollos, who before he became an apostle was "fervent in the spirit…knowing only the baptism of John" (Acts 18:25). Salvation is a process, not a one-time event. It begins with faith, only realized with obedience, and ends with endurance to the end.

It is true that I believe that the new birth of water and spirit means being baptized in water in the name of Jesus Christ and being baptized in the Holy Spirit. Why do I believe that? It is because of all the examples of water and spirit baptisms written in the Bible's history book of the church, Acts of the Apostles. Most all preachers of every denomination know these examples in Acts 2, Acts 8, Acts 10, and Acts 19. Why should any preacher apologize for preaching what is often spoken of as the plan of salvation from the Acts 2:38 perspective? However, others preach the Roman Road Plan, referring primarily to John 3:16 and to the book of Romans. None should apologize for preaching salvation from those scriptures as well. The fact is that each of these scriptures—those found in John, Acts, or

Romans—is equally true, but what makes preaching false, as told in Revelation 22, is that which is added in or that which is left out (Revelation 22:18–19). Here is the greatest admonition that I can give to any preacher: preach the Word. If there is a doctrine, a holiness standard, or a subject that is questionable, be sure it is covered in the Word of God, for we have this assurance:

> All scripture is given by inspiration of God, and is profitable for doctrine, for reproof, for correction, for instruction in righteousness: That the man of God may be perfect, thoroughly furnished unto all good works. (2 Timothy 3:16–17)

Whatever is needed to be preached is covered in the book, and going outside of the book is only going to create confusion and division.

Avoiding False Judgment

As a young boy, I went to a private Christian school that put strong emphasis on the name of the church denomination. I won't go through my whole testimony here, but like many other Christians, I did my share of church shopping. At some point in time, I realized that if the Lord had told his people what name needed to be on the church door, the devil would paint a sign and put it in front of the church. But one preacher so wisely stated, "It is not the name on the door that makes the difference. It is the doctrine in the pulpit and the experience in the pew that matters when it comes to the church."

In 1997, Grady wrote for *Charisma* magazine, "There are 17 million of them in the world, but Oneness Pentecostals are not even considered Christians by some in the church. Who are these people, and why have they been labeled heretics for more than 80 years."[15]

[15.] J. Lee Grady, "The Other Pentecostals," *Charisma Magazine* (June 1967): 62–63.

The article was passionate, but accurate, as Grady attempted to explain what he called a tough theological issue—that is, "The Other Pentecostals," who are known as apostolics or Jesus Only or Oneness Pentecostals and that now number many more millions in every corner of the globe. The following statements by *Charisma* tell it all:

> "Labeled heretics in 1916, these people have lived in isolation ever since" (p. 62). He continues, "Though Oneness Pentecostals believe in the deity of Christ and the authority of scripture, their rejection of Trinitarian terminology and their rigid position on baptism (in Jesus name) have put them in an awkward position. They are too orthodox to be compared to Mormons or Jehovah's Witness, yet they are too sectarian to mix with other evangelicals. So no one really knows what to do with them."[16]

However, the point is that all in ministry, regardless of denomination, have the obligation to take responsibility for their own teaching. It is unwise to see the Christian church as one denomination that is inerrant in any of its understanding and doctrinal position, or absolutely infallible when it comes to having truth. The truth is that all Christian and Jewish denominations are made up of humans that are imperfect. The word *perfect* from the Greek word *telios* means "complete," so conversely, *imperfect* means "incomplete," which means that we only know what we know, and we don't know what we don't know. Paul wisely stated,

> For we know in part, and we prophesy in part. But when that which is perfect is come, then that which is in part shall be done away. When I was a child, I spake as a child, I understood as a child, I thought as a child: but when I became a man, I

---

16. Grady, 63.

put away childish things. For now we see through
a glass, darkly; but then face to face: now I know
in part; but then shall I know even as also I am
known. (1 Corinthians 13:9–12)

When Paul said, "For we know in part," and then, "For we see
through a glass darkly" he was admitting what each of us should
admit. None of us has it all. The height of ignorance is to remain
ignorant while saying, "I am always right." Certainly each of us that
minister is expected to know the "truth that makes us free"—that
is, the gospel of Jesus Christ—and as I said before, most Christian
ministers preach the death, burial, and resurrection of Jesus Christ,
which is the gospel, but it is what is added in or taken out that creates
perversion. Paul condemned the Jewish Christians, not for being circumcised, but for adding it into the gospel as a requirement for salvation. Others who preach the gospel have taken out those things that
are required for salvation, such as repentance, water baptism, holy
spirit baptism, holiness—the things that are part of the obedience
aspect of salvation and make up the basic foundational doctrines of
the church (Hebrews 6:1–2). Others add in requirements that may
include anything from an issue on holiness to an issue over eating
habits, while at the same time taking out things that God wants left
in to fulfill his purposes in the church. This latter, I believe, sadly
includes the fivefold gifts of ministry and the gifts of the spirit.

The caution for all of us who minister is to recognize that the
basic and simple message of the gospel—that is, preaching the death,
burial, and resurrection of Jesus Christ—by itself does not complete the salvation process, but as Paul gave thanks that it was being
preached even when for the wrong reason, we must not become
judges of those in other denominations, neither must we neglect
being sure of how or why we are ministers of Jesus Christ. All of us
lack understanding in something.

Paul told Timothy, Till I come, give attendance
to reading, to exhortation, to doctrine. Neglect
not the gift that is in thee, which was given thee

by prophecy, with the laying on of the hands of the presbytery. Meditate upon these things; give thyself wholly to them; that thy profiting may appear to all. Take heed unto thyself, and unto the doctrine; continue in them: for in doing this thou shalt both save thyself, and them that hear thee. (1 Timothy 4:13–16)

Paul also wrote,

Study to shew thyself approved unto God, a workman that needeth not to be ashamed, rightly dividing the word of truth. But shun profane and vain babblings: for they will increase unto more ungodliness. And their word will eat as doth a canker: of whom is Hymenaeus and Philetus; Who concerning the truth have erred, saying that the resurrection is past already; and overthrow the faith of some. (2 Timothy 2:15–18)

But foolish and unlearned questions avoid, knowing that they do gender strifes. And the servant of the Lord must not strive; but be gentle unto all *men*, apt to teach, patient, In meekness instructing those that oppose themselves; if God peradventure will give them repentance to the acknowledging of the truth; And *that* they may recover themselves out of the snare of the devil, who are taken captive by him at his will. (2 Timothy 2:23–28)

What is the point of all that I am saying? First, I am writing to preachers. Second, I am writing not only to preachers of the organization or denomination that I belong to as a minister but to all preachers in the Christian faith. Third, my purpose is to explain how our imperfect human nature is such a reality that I am hoping I can influence my reading audience to weigh heavily the following proposition: neither you nor I are absolutely perfect in truth or understanding and must leave open that in many areas of our preaching, we can sincerely be wrong about something. It does not mean that we will necessarily lose our souls, although if we are wrong in the wrong thing, we could. But it does mean that we must stay open-minded enough and be willing enough to continually search the scripture, be determined to rightly divide the Word of Truth, and if need be, humbly change our way of doing things, if we are understanding changes. Do not let tradition or even culture dictate a set-in-stone way of doing things if we see it does not comport to the Word and Spirit of God. No license, no denomination, and no relationship with others should keep us from doing those things that align with the four elements that are essentials to fulfilling the purposes of God's calling for us as ministers: the mission (purpose), the brand (message), the culture (ministry), and the methods that God set forth to doing the work of the church.

CHAPTER 6

Church Polity

The term for church government is *polity*, which generally takes one of three forms: Episcopal, Presbyterian, or Congregational. In addition to these three traditional forms is the single-pastor-led congregation. Also, to be considered in the concept of government are forms that pertain to power structures. Even though there are structural differences in the definitions of polity, the use of power can vary in leadership styles within any one of the forms of government.

The original model of church government has evolved—first, through the selection of plural elders; and later, the selection of one of the elders into a position that acted as the chairman of the board. In the latter form, the leading elder seldom operated independent of other elders or other forms of accountability. Most of this accountability would have been locally self-contained, depending on the structure of collegial eldership in the local church where several elders would be accountable to one another. The allocation of power and influence ultimately depends on interpersonal dynamics, but under a collegial model, positional authority is initially dispersed.

During the first century, and because of distance separation and no formal organization, local church leaders were independent of higher authorities. However, they were influenced and guided by apostolic letters and apostolic visits. The instructions to Timothy and Titus for elder qualifications were of utmost importance because local church elders were primarily left to their own devices for the day-to-day operation of the church. Elders must be spirit filled and spirit led, with full vertical accountability to God. However, God in his wisdom did not set aside horizontal accountability, where leaders must be accountable to other leaders—and all members of the body accountable to one another.

The expansion of missions and church planting contributed to changes in polity in several ways. While the original Jerusalem church provided a semblance of structural hierarchy, its influence was limited to pronouncements, as in the Acts 15 conference, and guidance from emissaries, whether apostles or others who were sent out to visit the scattered churches. Time and distance were such that close observation or oversight of local churches were impossible. As it is today, church government is on a continuum with the strongest axis of leadership being contained within the local congregation itself and many with a form of positional authority vested in a sole pastor with diminished authority allocated to a board or other ministries.

Chute writes, "Polity may not be a popular topic in an 'anti-institutional age,' but it is foundational to the local church."[17] With the increasing number of churches that identify as nondenominational, at least in the United States, there is the semblance of a rejection of traditional hierarchical styles of leadership cloaked in the guise of "we do not want doctrine." Nondenominational rhetoric is the rejection of being identified with dogmas, doctrines, or religious forms that are associated with a specific denominational brand. The "brand" of religion is based on doctrinal assertions, leadership styles, and the cultural rules that are a part of the church tradition. It is not out-of-hand rejection of the gospel message or of God but of the confusion that exist in conflicting multiple messages. Chute contends that the anti-institutional sentiment that shies away from issues of church government are because the subject "implies authority and invites division."[18]

[17.] Anthony Chute, "Baptist Foundations: Church Government for an Anti-institutional Age," *Baptist History and Heritage* 51, no. 2 (2016): 94+. *General OneFile* (accessed March 15, 2019), https://link.galegroup.com/apps/doc/A468140934/GPS?u=fl_program&sid=GPS&xid=4b71fe31.

[18.] Chute, 397.

Episcopalian Polity

Episcopalian church government is hierarchical in structure, where a group of local churches (diocese) are overseen by one who is known as a bishop or presiding bishop, while the local church has a priest or rector as its minister of sacraments, including the homilies. The term *bishop* is from the Greek *episkopay*, as used in 1 Timothy 3:1 and again in Titus 1:5–7. Note that the term *bishop* and *elder* are synonymous in Paul's letter to Titus, which means the Episcopalian form is structurally different in that it creates a hierarchy that removes at least a portion of power that was to be vested in the elders of the local church.

While it may seem that that the episcopal form of bishop/elder seems to draw support from scripture, the practice of top-down authority means that there are levels of authority that extend upward to what at one time was the papacy of Roman Catholicism—or in this modern day, to organizational hierarchy. The local power within the church is minimal in comparison and functions at the behest of higher power structures. The historical change from the pope to an archbishop under the English king Henry VIII (1509–1547) is controversial because King Henry likely did not intend that the English church would differ in polity structure except for its rejection of the Roman pope.

The modern structure of bishops, priests, and deacons in the English form was modified in the American system to add a congregational element, a result of the American Revolution. In the United States, the bishop leaders who have power and authority are limited by the laity of the congregation, which serve as delegates to conventions that establish policy. This system of checks and balances was modeled much like the structure of the American government. Butler (1995) writes,

> In the year following the Revolution, American Anglicans were concerned about the structure of an Episcopal church and the role of bishops within that structure. Episcopalians faced a perplexing

59

problem of church government. Most of the states reorganized their churches around a plan of confederation proposed by William White, in which traditional terminology from bishops was avoided and replaced by "overseer," "president," and "superior order." These overseers would share authority with clergy and lay delegates in a convention.[19]

The bishops were considered to have pastoral care and authority related to those duties, but the direction of the church in the United States is heavily influenced by the laity. The result is the changing social and political climate that has fractured the leadership of the church and created divisions within the body of churches that are Episcopalian in polity.

Presbyterian Polity

Presbyterian polity is another form of elder rule, but the elders in local bodies are less a ruling class of clergy than a ruling class of laity—and a representative form of government. In effect, a Presbyterian polity is a form of oligarchy, which means that power is vested in a small group of people rather than a single individual. An oligarchy contrasts with a dictatorship in terms of sharing the power base. Dictatorships and monarchies typically refer to autonomous rule mostly associated with an autocracy, which is rule by one person. Few churches go that far because churchgoing is voluntary and such power cannot be enforced by man except when it takes on a cultic identity, which is the underlying danger of what I have described as the pastoral supremacy syndrome when extremes develop in the behaviors of a single leader.

In the discussion of the Episcopal form, it should be noted that the American church, in which lay delegates have greater influ-

---

[19.] Diana H. Butler, *Standing Against the Whirldwind: Evangelical Espiscopalians in Nineteenth-Century America* (New York: Oxford University Press, 1995).

ence, moved church polity away from the strictest form of Episcopal rule toward a Presbyterian form, the difference being that under the Presbyterian polity, the church board (or assembly of representatives) has greater power than the ministry ordained by God. Presbyters are generally elected by the local churches and act as delegates to the General Assembly in setting church policy. Graham (1996) notes that Thomas Witherow (1824–1890) of Scotland identified six basic principles of Presbyterianism. These include the following:

- Office bearers are chosen by the people
- The offices of bishop and elder are identical
- A plurality of elders in each church
- Ordination was the act of the presbytery
- There was a privilege of appeal to the elders for the right of the church to speak
- The only head of the church is Jesus Christ[20]

These six principles closely model scriptural principles with the exception that ordaining elders in the Bible was not a matter of voting by the congregation but by ordination from apostles and elders (Titus 1:5, Acts 14:23). This is a significant point to be discussed later. In addition, within scripture it appears that the elders and leadership of the church were represented more by the preaching ministry (i.e., fivefold ministry), rather than by a congregational laity (1 Timothy 5:17, Acts 13:1–3). Presbyterianism is best described as a representative form of government, which is not in keeping with the implications of scripture. Biblical ordination by apostles and elders suggests an apostolic succession associated with the conferring of ministerial gifts rather than the conferring of positional authority (1 Timothy 4:14).

While Presbyterianism is in one aspect a form of congregational rule, it differs from Congregationalist polity in that the arbiter of church policy and rule exists in the representatives of an assembly

---

20. Ross Graham, "The Biblical Origins of the Presbytery," *Ordained Servant* 5 (1996): 2, https://www.opc.org/OS/html/V5/2f.html.

that is higher than the local church. Presbyters are grouped in synods, which in turn are joined together on a nationwide basis in their general assembly. Authority flows from top to bottom, from the assembly to the local. Only a presbytery can ordain ministers, install pastors, or make changes in opening, closing, or relocating churches.

Congregational Polity

Congregational polity does not necessarily mean that the congregation is the final authority in the local church. While the local church might be ruled by a body of local elders or by a single pastor, the polity refers to the overall authority that rests in the local church and moves from bottom to top when local churches are joined in fellowship or denominational structure. Under congregational polity, the power structure in the laity is often at odds with the pastoral ministry. This gives rise to one of the major complaints of pastors—that the shepherd becomes a "hireling." Many such churches are autonomous and independent, and whether the local church follows the rules of a church organization is done on a selective basis. Most of the time, local churches will pick and choose what will be followed, and much of the choosing is determined by whatever power structure exists in the local church. It is not unusual for many evangelical churches to have congregational power structures that are represented by family dynasties.

Oligarchy Polity

An oligarchy can exist under the concept of eldership in which a few elders have all the power within a congregation. An oligarchy can also exist within any of the church polity structures mentioned. What has caused pastors consternation and fear is the board of elders that turn the preacher into a "hireling" and control the man and the message. The possibility that church leaders have intermediaries between them and the head of the church, Jesus Christ, is the most dangerous form of government. Church leaders, whether preacher or not, must be in direct relationship with Jesus Christ, the King of kings. This highlights the importance of understanding God's biblical model for leadership.

Most single-pastor forms of church structure are simply a matter of one oligarchy that replaces another oligarchy. The pastor and inner circle replace the "elders," a form where elders rule the church. Such an oligarch is often the pastor and pastor's family, or a dynasty that develops over time. While this may be natural (see "Founder's Syndrome"), it is not the concept of "few" that is problematic—it is the perception and use of authority and power that are the cause for alarm. Under collegial eldership, authority and power is dispersed, meaning no one in the structure has sole authority except for Jesus Christ.

The reality is that whether a church is an oligarchy, collegial rule, single-pastor rule, or any of the other forms of church government, the potential for abuse is always present. This book is not primarily about "government" but about the fivefold ministry, which should be active in any form of church government. It is true, there is scriptural evidence that strongly supports the principle of multiple elders and deacons as the office bearers for church government. Why this structure exists is the bigger question. What is suggested is that church government is not about positional power and authority but about the execution of ministry and service. Those that are to be ordained as office bearers of elders and deacons were most often identified in scripture as those who had one of the ministerial gifts.

Very little is written about the fivefold ministry as the true expression of power and authority in the church. Instead authority is identified almost exclusively in the term *pastor* or *elder*, and the meanings of those terms are not synonymous, even though this is the perception in this modern era. *Elder* is a term denoting authority, and *pastor* is a term denoting servitude, as in a caretaker position. The problem is that both now have been combined and used to the exclusion of the other gifts of service (Ephesians 4), and both terms are now reflected in what has been reinforced in church polity—a traditional meaning that *government* means the exercise of authority and power to "control," rather than to "serve."

CHAPTER 7

Power Structures

Leadership as a subset of organizational studies is characterized in terms of styles, traits, behaviors, and roles and like all great theories is a complex subject that engenders years of research, discussion, and debate. Leadership theories and organizational theories can seldom be discussed as separate issues because organizations entail vertical and horizontal relationships. As much as anything else, leadership is about relationship. The structures of organizations often mirror the style of the leaders. Formal organizations may have a strong hierarchical structure, and this suggests that the structure was put in place and is maintained by leaders that also perceive leadership in terms of hierarchy. Organizations can also be informal, which fosters a more cooperative style of relationship—such as social networks or communities of common interest—and these also reflect perceptions of leadership styles. This suggests that there is a correlation between how leadership develops and how organizations develop as a result of forms of leadership.

Williams (2012) writes, "Organizational structure is the vertical and horizontal configuration of departments, authority, and jobs with a company" (p. 250).[21] It refers to how relationships are structured, how authority is distributed, and how work gets accomplished.

[21.] Charles Williams, *Effective Management*, 6th (Mason, OH: South-Western Cengage Learning, 2012).

Marak (1964) notes leadership structure refers both to relationship and to an authority-compliance configuration that defines the nature of the relationship. Marak writes, "The development of a leadership structure—an asymmetry in the relative frequencies of control and compliance acts initiated and received by the members of a group—depends upon a situation in which one person has more power than another" (p. 175).[22] The structural configuration, whether vertical or horizontal, weak or strong, close or distant, can say a lot about the dynamics of the relationship.

Marak (1964) notes, "Possessions, personality, and position in a social structure are interrelated variables that influence the evolution of control-compliance interaction patterns."[23] This telling comment reveals a great deal about the nature and purpose of power. Why does anyone want to be a leader? This begs the question as to whether leadership equates to power or authority—and does power infer the promise of reward, as in greater position or more possessions? Typically the concept of leadership is enthroned in the notion of status, position, or other personal benefits. It is a given that team leaders at a fast-food restaurant receive a wage increase when promoted even if it only means a quarter an hour difference. Middle managers have compensating rewards, and top managers are endued with even greater rewards. The conceptualization of what leaders do and what leaders are has a cultural perspective associated with power and rewards that distort the real understanding of leadership.

Configurations of Power

The uncomfortable truth is that power, position, and possessions are interrelated factors in human social context. Note the change from Marak's triad of social structure variables, where we substitute power for personality in a discussion of the real-world configura-

---

[22]. George E. Marak, "The Evolution of Leadership Structures," *Sociometry* 27, no. 2 (June 1964): 174–182.
[23]. Marak, 175.

tions of which we are culturally familiar. Social structures are relevant to multidisciplinary studies of sociology, psychology, organizational theory, natural sciences, and even theology. In general, any subject dealing with how things relate to one another must consider structural configurations. Structural configurations suggest position in the configuration, and how things are positioned suggests ways that we can discuss elements of power, control, status, or influence. These are elements of elite circles of influence that for many say, "I have arrived," or that are associated with notions of achievement. Dogan (2003) in the book *Introduction: Diversity of Elite Configurations and Clusters of Power* writes,

> The notion of configuration which appears in the title of this book has the same meaning as in astronomy: the position of planetary corps in relation to one another. In elite studies, configuration means the relative position and size of various elite circles (political, bureaucratic, capitalist, managerial, cultural, religious, military, etc.) in the constellation of power.[24]

Elitism entails symbols that become expectations in terms of cultural power distance. The term *power distance* refers "to the extent to which the members of a culture are willing to accept an unequal distribution of power, wealth, and prestige."[25] The authors also note that high-power-distance cultures like Brazil, Singapore, or Arabic countries rely heavily on hierarchy in their power structures. High power distance is structured vertically, with more power at the top, where subordinates expect to be told what to do. Low-power-distance cultures are more democratic and imply a horizontal distribution of power, which is shared between managers and subordinates. "As a

---

[24.] Mattei Dogan, "Introduction: Diversity of Elite Configurations and Clusters of Power," *Comparative Sociology* 2, no. 1 (2003): 1.

[25.] Mary J. Hatch and Ann L. Cuntliffe, *Organization Theory: Modern, Symbolic, and Postmodern Perspectives, ed. 2* (Oxford, NY: Oxford University Press, 2006), 181.

consequence of these contradictory expectations, the ideal boss in a low power distance culture is a resourceful democrat, whereas in a high-power distance culture the best boss is a benevolent autocrat."[26]

Clearly power relationships are culturally relevant, normal, and necessary. The whole notion of "law" is based on relationships of power and authority. Without law, there is no order, and anarchy suggests the breaking down of power structures that are intended to provide safety and harmony to social structures. The etymology of the word *power* from the Anglo-French *pouair* and the Latin *potis* defines power as "ability, ability to act or do; strength, vigor, might, efficacy, control, mastery, dominion, authority"—many synonyms that can have very positive meanings associated with accomplishment and achievement ("Power," *Online Etymology Dictionary*). Power, however, is a two-edged sword, either to be feared or revered, not for the fact of its existence, but only because of its consequences. A well-known quotation by Baron John Acton states, "Power tends to corrupt, and absolute power corrupts absolutely. Great men are almost always bad men" (Aston, The Phrase Finder, n.d.).

On the other hand, the apostle Paul declares power as a role of government, not to be feared, but to be respected. Paul writes,

> Let every soul be subject unto the higher powers. For there is no power but of God: the powers that be are ordained of God. Whosoever therefore resisteth the power resisteth the ordinance of God: and they that resist shall receive to themselves damnation. For rulers are not a terror to good works, but to the evil. Wilt thou then not be afraid of the power? do that which is good, and thou shalt have praise of the same. (Romans 13:1–3, KJV)

I would argue the symbols most associated with power, position, and possessions are not necessary to power. It has been said that power tends to corrupt, and if so, does this mean that power itself is

---

[26.] Hatch and Cuntliffe, 183.

of a corrupting nature? This would certainly not be the view of Paul, nor as we shall see is it a biblical view from understanding the many scriptures that elevate power as characterized by "ability"—for example, "And when he had called unto him his twelve disciples, he gave them power against unclean spirits, to cast them out, and to heal all manner of sickness and all manner of disease" (Matthew 10:1).

We hypothesize that it is not power that corrupts, but rather position and possessions are what corrupt those that have power. Power without love is the most dangerous form of power, and since love, other than for self, suggests the opposite of self-interest, power that is noncorrupting can only be power not driven by self-interest.

Leadership versus Power

It is important to distinguish between power and leadership. The term *power* refers to authority and control; leadership refers to influence, and although this is a form of power, leadership does not necessarily result from authority or control. The earlier mention of distortion concerning leadership is significant because there is a tendency in human nature to look to positional power for leadership, and this is the root cause of "the blind leading the blind"[27] syndrome (Matthew 15:14). The corporate struggle for position on the ladder of success often equates to the part of the triad in our discussion—possessions—but is also about a desire for positional power. Real leadership, however, is not bound by position or possessions but has influence as its own form of power.

Influence can come from beneath one's own status and gives rise to the concept of servant leaders. Every teacher, manager, parent, or governor is wise to listen to those who have subordinate roles. The reality is that influence is a powerful two-way street that "leads" others to action, whether good or bad. Because leaders do for the most part excel to positions of power, it is normal to view leadership equating to power in a relationship. The nuanced difference is that

---

[27.] Matthew 15:14, KJV.

leadership in the context of influence suggests that it has more to do with the powers of personality and influence, while concepts of control are based on the powers of position and possessions—for example, the "power of the purse." The characterization of a servant leader implies that position, possessions, and status are not what make the servant leader. The servant leader can influence from roles suggested by subordinates: a student, a child, a subordinate worker, or one who is governed—meaning the obedient servant of another. The servant leader uses a frame of mind for him- or herself and a frame of reference in the eyes of the subordinate that whatever influences the leader has, they are for the benefit of the subordinate, not the leader.

Servant Leadership

Servant leadership is a leadership style that focuses on building relationships and leading from core values of care, concern, and charity (love). Kent Keith posits that with so much advice available about leadership, new leaders should start with the basic principles of servant leadership[28] (2009, p. 18). This means that leaders should strengthen relationships with their colleagues. These three principles begin with "go to work to serve others" (p. 18). This is the real reason why leadership roles exist. The leader that believes leadership is "all about the leader" is missing the point about relationship and influence.

A second basic part of servant leadership is that leaders must "listen to colleagues and customers to identify and meet their needs."[29] The servant leader operates as a mentor, guide, counselor, adviser, and sharer of vision. Terry Bean, an old colleague of mine, had great insight into understanding relationships by simply asking the question, "Whose needs are being met?" Kent suggests that a servant

---

[28] Kent M. Keith, "Servant Leaders Observe Three Basic Principles," *Leadership Excellence Essentials* 26, no. 5 (May 2009): 18–19, http://ezproxy.liberty.edu/login?url=http://search.ebscohost.com/login.aspx?direct=true&db=bth&AN=39555734&site=ehost-live&scope=site.

[29] Keith, 18.

leader should not begin with their own answers but be first asking others about their needs, wants, and desires (2009, p. 18). Servant leaders focus on the value of the relationship to those they lead.

Third, servant leaders "develop colleagues," says Keith.[30] If leadership exists because of a relationship, growth in leadership comes with growth in the relationship. Many good leaders fail by working themselves out of a job. Kent is writing about servant leadership in the context of sales when he says, "Your ability to serve customers will only be as good as your colleagues," but the basic principle is that your efforts at leadership are always measured by the results of others. Whether the metric is production, achievement, or sales dollars, it reflects back to the leader, who gets the recognition for the group. Servant leaders grow the value of their own leadership by leading others into the realm of success.

The Difference of Servant Leadership

Leadership structures in religious communities are varied in accordance with differences in ecclesiastical views of church polity. The traditional views of church government—Episcopal, Presbyterian, or Congregational—continue to exist, but modern forms include the single-pastor-led church, democratic congregation-led churches, or forms of plural leadership. While leadership structure in a religious community may vary, it must be conceded that each of the different models work given the right conditions; and for that reason, they continue to exist. This is true of churches and businesses, and a discussion of which form works best is the purview of leadership studies. Here we hypothesize that the concept of servant leadership as a characteristic of leadership is unique in that it is culturally oxymoronic. The power of the servant leader is amplified by its very nature of standing out in contrast to how humans typically view power—and this contrast engages the human heart into becoming willing followers in a relationship with that special meaning of "being different from all the rest."

[30.] Keith, 19.

The Jesus Model: Inverted Authority

Jesus understood the nature of jealousy and self-interest and addressed it early with his disciples. When the mother of James and John came to Jesus and asked that her sons be seated next to Jesus in heaven, the other disciples were offended (Matthew 20:20–28, KJV).

Jesus then contrasted his concept of leadership with the known leadership of the day:

> Ye know that the princes of the Gentiles exercise dominion over them, and they that are great exercise authority upon them. But it shall not be so among you: but whosoever will be great among you, let him be your minister. (Matthew 20:25–26, KJV)

In the book *Restoring the Fivefold Ministry*, this is called inverted authority, which is the kind of authority required for leadership in the church.[31] It is a servant-leader model that is recognized in the business world as well as the church world. Emma De Vita sums up a quote from a little-known book *Servant-Leadership*, stating, "True leaders must also be servants. Great leaders must serve their communities and earn loyalty by involvement rather than imposition."[32] "Servant leadership," a phrase coined by Robert Greenleaf, is a concept that influenced Stephen Covey's book *The 7 Habits of Highly Successful People* and John Carver's *Boards That Make A Difference (Cassel & Holt)*.[33] But the concept originated with God when he dethroned Moses to make him the leader of the children of Israel.[34]

31. Hartwell Paul Davis, *Restoring the Five Fold Ministry* (2004), p. 2.
32. Emma DeVita, "Servant Leadership," Third Sector (September 24, 2008), 25. Retrieved from https://www.thirdsector.co.uk/theory-servant-leadership/communications/article/848028.
33. J. Cassell and T. Holt, "The Servant Leader," *American School Board Journal* 195, no. 10 (October 2008): 34–35. Retrieved from Academic Source Complete Database.
34. Davis, p. 3.

CHAPTER 8

The Earliest Power Structures

A discussion of servant leadership often includes the Matthew
20:25–27 text, in which Jesus states to his disciple,

> But Jesus called them unto him, and said, Ye
> know that the princes of the Gentiles exercise
> dominion over them, and they that are great exer-
> cise authority upon them. But it shall not be so
> among you: but whosoever will be great among
> you, let him be your minister; And whosoever
> will be chief among you, let him be your servant.

However, the concept of power structures began in Genesis 2 in
the creation story. Leadership, authority, control, prestige, and power
are normal elements in structures of relationships. There are few, if
any, structures that can claim complete equality for all members, and
it is the concept of equality that creates the tension that exists in any
power relationship.

Here is an opportunity to create a veritable firestorm by stating that "equality issues" are dangerous grounds for our discussion
because we posit that biblical text does not suggest total gender equality in male-female relationships, specifically in the context of marriage. Nor does it prohibit equality in many areas of life. Power and
equality can never be taken in concepts of totality with the exception

of only one omnipotent being, God, who has all power, and nothing is equal to him. All issues of power and equality must be in the context of their structural determinations. To reiterate, the nature of the structure and the nature of the relationships in the structure determine the types, the limits, and the distributions of power.

Obviously the question concerns "equal in what way or not equal in what way"? Semantic issues require exegetical and textual analysis to "rightly divide the word of truth" in matters of gender relationships. The relationship between husband and wife, which is the first biblical reference for power relationships, is from Genesis, which reads, "Then he [sic God] said to the woman, 'I will sharpen the pain of your pregnancy, and in pain you will give birth. And you will desire to control your husband, but he will rule over you'" (Genesis 2:18, New Literal Translation).

Prior to this pronouncement as the result of the fall of man, we shall consider an earlier biblical text that in our English language suggests a structural configuration that appears to be vertical in nature in that the term "helper" refers to an assistant or attendant. The pericope in Genesis states, "Then the Lord God said it was not good for man to be alone. I will make a helper who is just right for him." McGlone (1989) notes, "The word translated 'helper' is literally 'one corresponding to him.'"[35] The exegesis should consider two questions about the original context of the power relationship.

The first question is, do the texts support a vertical structure by using the word *helper*? The context that follows states, "And Adam said, This is now bone of my bones, and flesh of my flesh: she shall be called Woman, because she was taken out of Man. Therefore shall a man leave his father and his mother, and shall cleave unto his wife: and they shall be one flesh" (Genesis 2:23–24, KJV). The emphatic statement of relationship in that the woman and the man are "one flesh" suggests not two existing in a relationship side by side but two becoming one being that "makes or completes" the whole man. This is in keeping with the very definition of *woman*—"taken out of man." The marriage relationship is a restorative function—the

---

[35.] Lee McGlone, *Review and Expositor* 86: p. 244.

inference of one flesh meaning completion. In the sense of being "one," the relationship of two is replaced by the completeness of one, which in effect removes the structure of two—and hence, any power relationship.

Viewed from a structure of one, there would exist no power structure. The term *equal* is not relevant when one can equal nothing else but one. We interject that *equal* refers to a concept in which there are two or more elements. It is easy to understand why God states, "To whom then will you liken me, or shall I be equal," or, "To whom will you compare me, who is my equal" (Isaiah 46:5, KJV). The fact that there is only one God means there is no equal and equality is a moot point. In creation, when God made man and woman "one flesh," he removed the structure of two and any semblance of power structure.

The second question in the analysis is if man and woman are "one" in the original meaning, therefore without a power relationship, where do we then find the suggestion of man's power over the woman. The answer is in the pronouncement of Genesis 3, after the fall—as a result of sin that changed not only the nature of man's oneness with God but man's nature of oneness with his wife. Sin created the divides that made structural changes between God, man, and woman. Sin necessitated the need for power structures, which resulted in *law* for the "God and man" structure and *headship* or *covering* in the "man and woman" structure. The concept of headship as a power structure is covered by Paul in 1 Corinthians (man and woman—1 Corinthians 11:1–13, KJV), in Ephesians (Ephesians 1:22, 4:15, 5:23), and Colossians (Christ and the church—Colossians 1:18, 2:10, 2:19).

The notion of equality implies a state where authority or power does not exist between equal members, and biblical text does not preclude gender equality in most areas of life. This is the reason for the confusion that gave rise to feminist theology. What is most often missed in the discussion of power is that the nature of the relationship determines the extent, purpose, and constructs of the power in the relationship, and the Genesis 3:16 pericope must be taken in the context of what happened in the fall of man that precipitated the power structure. The woman was deceived by Satan, ate of the tree of knowledge of good and evil, and enticed her husband to do the same. The resulting spiritual condition caused God to create spiritual authority, power, or control for the purposes of protection against further spiritual attack.

Note Paul's explanation for the power structure in the 1 Corinthians 11 pericope concerning headship: "For this cause ought the woman to have power on her head because of the angels" (1 Corinthians 11:10, KJV). Paul writes, "And Adam was not deceived, but the woman being deceived was in the transgression" (1 Timothy 2:14, KJV). The nature of the woman is to be more spiritually sensitive than the man. It is not uncommon for women and children to often make up the greater portion of church congregations. The woman's spiritual sensitivity is a positive in a relationship with God, but as a negative, it enhances her vulnerability to Satan's attack. For this reason, man's rule over the woman from Genesis 3:16 is seen by Paul in the context of spiritual warfare. It is not seen in the context of domination over other areas of her life.

Only God has all power; for the rest of us, power is intended to have boundaries and limits. In a husband-wife relationship, for example, God gave man the power to protect his wife, but not the power to prevent his wife from being successful in business. One only has to read a few scriptures to understand that women may have financial privileges. Solomon writes,

> Who can find a virtuous and capable wife? She is more precious than rubies. Her husband can trust her, and she will greatly enrich his life. She brings him good not harm, all the days of her life. She finds wool and flax and busily spins it. She is like a merchant's ship, bringing her food from afar. She gets up before dawn to prepare breakfast for her household and plan the day's work for her servant girls. She goes to inspect a field and buys it; with her earnings she plants a vineyard. She is energetic and strong, a hard worker. She makes sure her dealings

are profitable; her lamp burns late into the night.
(Proverbs 31:10–18, New Literal Translation)

Here the woman is described as being capable, involved in business, and making "sure her dealings are profitable."

A second scripture speaks of the women that were disciples of Jesus who supported him: "Among them were Mary Magdalene, from whom he had cast out seven demons; Joanna, the wife of Chuza, Herod's business manager; Susanna; and many others who were contributing their own resources to support Jesus and his disciples" (Luke 8:1–3, NLT). The "many others" could suggest that this included men, but it is evident by the mention of the women, there was parity for women in the social structure during the time of Jesus.

The danger of feminist theology is that if the relationship was created where the power element was intended for safety, security, and order, equality in essence removes the power, thus removing the safety that was intended. We posit that safety, security, and order are the purposes for the Genesis 3 power relationship, that it is specific to the marriage relationship, and that other elements often associated with power—namely, possessions, positions outside of marriage, wealth, or prestige—are not included by God in the power structure envisioned in the said chapter.

Unfortunately, the feminist view of the Genesis 3 pericope about the creation of man and woman misses entirely the power elements being discussed in the passage, and it takes analysis of several texts written by Apostle Paul to have a better understanding of the power relationship between man and woman that was intended by God. The fact that feminists have missed the point of the Genesis pericope has opened up the dangers of feminist theology, discussed later. In the context of Genesis 2 and 3, we will confine the discussion to suggesting the following hypotheses:

1. Not all structural relations are power relationships. In terms of power, the notion of horizontal relationship conceptualizes the absence of power between horizontal members. Note this does not

conceptualize absence of influence if we are discussing power in reference to authority and control.

2. If the structural relationship includes a power relationship element, shifting to equality changes the structure and cancels the purpose of the power element.

3. If the elements of power and control are intended to provide safety and security, equality removes the power mechanisms that provided safety and security.

What must be considered in the discussion is that power is a two-edged sword in all cultures, where on the one hand power increases wealth and prestige for the powerful and is often used to inhibit or at least control wealth and prestige for others. This is positive for those in power and negative for those subject to power. At the same time, power is used in maintaining order, which is reflected in matters of safety and security, this being a positive use of power.

Power therefore can be viewed both positively and negatively and is the most central element of any conflict. When God created the relationship between man and woman, God also created positional power that has been maligned and misinterpreted and has engendered some of the greatest debates about the nature of power and control. The issue of gender equality is of such significance that it has sparked a worldwide conflagration that has fanned the flames of social engineering, women's rights, and, yes, gay rights. Hatch and Cunliffe (2006) observe,

> A number of feminist scholars have argued that this separation of male and female domains and practices reinforces a binary view of gender that underpins the everyday actions and interactions of both men and women, thus repro-

ducing traditional relations of domination and subordination.[36]

To the feminist, male and female relationships—particularly a traditional view of the relationship—are all about power and domination. David DeSilva notes, "Basic to feminist criticism is a rejection of patriarchy—an ideology in which men and the male agenda are privileged and empowered, while women and the female agenda are relegated to ancillary roles."[37] The tragedy is the extent to which the ideology has created its own form of abuse by destroying the first and most primary of man's relationships.

Servant Leadership: The Perception of Equality

The assumption of all things being equal in any team sport is a myth, considering that differences in contribution usually result in differences in reward—even if it is limited to who gets the most media attention. It may be possible to design a relationship around equal authority, but it is unlikely that members of any relationship have equal influence. Leaders stand out from the rest, which is why influence develops. Leaders may not always have the best ideas, for others in an organizational structure also have ideas, but these often go unnoticed. At times those with positional power have less influence—a fact that has a way of creating tension for managers—because leadership again is not about position. The unique characteristic of servant leadership is that it reframes the debate about power, control, and equality. Servant leadership is an exercise of influence that has the ability to work as other forms of power but does so by providing the perception of equality.

---

36. Mary J. Hatch and Ann L. Cunliffe, *Organization Theory: Modern, Symbolic, and Postmodern Perspectives*, 2nd ed. (Oxford, NY: Oxford University Press, 2006), 273.

37. David A. DeSilva, *An Introduction to the New Testament: Contexts, Methods & Ministry Formation* (Downers Grove, IL: Inter Varisty Press, 2004), 757.

The tension between power relationships and issues of equality is a major source of conflict, not only in the gender battles, but in issues of race, economics, class warfare, and styles of government. The immortal declaration "All men are created equal" is enthroned in the United States Declaration of Independence. What has been called a self-evident truth is true in the sense that in the eyes of the creator, equality exists. Paul writes, "In this new life, it doesn't matter if you are a Jew or a Gentile, circumcised or uncircumcised, barbaric, uncivilized, slave, or free. Christ is all that matters, and he lives in all of us" (Colossians 3:11, NLT). All of humanity exists in one horizontal relationship with one another but only under One God, who has power over us all. What is also true is that equality is the basic desire of the heart, and that is why it serves as the expression of the principle that has attracted the millions that have come to America seeking freedom.

However, equality and freedom are seen as natural enemies and are a main point of disagreement between capitalists and egalitarians. Vorster (2010) writes, "In capitalist economies that allow citizens the freedom to dispose of their wealth in a manner they think fit, distributions are often extremely unequal. Egalitarian economies, on the other hand, frequently degenerate into oppression or into the equal distribution of poverty.[38]" The reason that equality and freedom are natural enemies is not because they are opposite in nature. *Equality* in the minds of most means the freedom to be treated the same, and in the Declaration of Independence, the linguistic context suggests that meaning. But if everyone in a communistic society is equally poor, is that the kind of freedom one expects?

In the realm of social organizations, all men are not equal, nor will they ever be. To suggest otherwise is, dare we say it, to exhibit the height of ignorance. A world without power structures is untenable, and even in the utopian state of Jesus ruling the earth, we are told, "Blessed and holy are those who share in the first resurrection. For them the second death holds no power, but they will be priests

---

[38] Nico Vorster, "Are Freedom and Equality Natural Enemies? A Christian Theological Perspective," *Heythrop Journal* 51, 4 (2010): 594.

of God and of Christ and will reign with him a thousand years"
(Revelation 20:6, KJV). Vorster (2010) observes,

> Equality is not part of the created structure of
> the human being—as is the case with freedom—
> because all people are not created with the same
> talents and abilities. All inequalities are therefore
> not necessarily unjust. The fallacy of extreme
> egalitarianism lies therein that it confuses equality
> with sameness and tries to minimize individual
> differences by enforcing similarities upon people.
> Sameness and enforced homogeneity contradict
> the diversity of creation.[39]

A relationship in any social structure can never be about complete equality, complete sameness, or even sameness in influence.
People are simply different even when a lack of similarity is minuscule.
Servant leadership does not remove power, it does not make everyone equal, and it does not assure that everyone will be treated the same.
What servant leadership does is lead from the perspective of equality
and sameness by imposing on one's self the empathy that taps into the
heartfelt desire of the subordinate to be an equal with the leader. Such is
the case in the Matthew 20 statement by Jesus, where we have what has
become known as the Lord's expression of servant leadership.

The Biblical Concept of Servant Leadership

When the mother of James and John asked Jesus, "Let my two
sons sit in places of honor next to you, one on your right and one on
your left" (Matthew 20:21, New Literal Translation), she could have
been requesting status, but having been a disciple of Jesus herself, she
knew that Jesus was not all about power, prestige, or wealth. Jesus
was the model servant leader, and he stated this to be truth: "For even

---

[39.] Vorster, 601.

the Son of man came not to be served but to serve others and to give his life a ransom for others" (v. 28). Jesus's reply was not a rebuke to the wife of Zebedee but in the form of a clarification.

Servant leadership is primarily about attitudes and perceptions, because servant leaders are so often bosses, managers, and wielders of power as well as of influence. Boone and Makhani (2012) describe five necessary attitudes of a servant leader. Servant leaders "institutionalize the virtue of serving others first, not serving oneself."[40] This demonstrates the purpose of the relationship between the leaders and subordinates. Second, "He observes that we add value to others when we know and relate to what others value."[41] This demonstrates the potential of the relationship. Third, "Effective servant leaders share a common attitude that 'everyone is great at something' and it is their responsibility to help followers realize how they can apply whatever special talent(s) they can offer toward achievement of the organization's vision."[42] This demonstrates the perspective of the relationship. Fourth, "Leaders accept and act on the paradox of power: you become more powerful when you give your own power away."[43] This is the paradox of servant leadership. Last of all, "Servant leaders recognize that their success derives from the attitude that they are leading an organizational effort to develop a productive community."[44] This is the end product of a servant leader relationship.

The nature of servant leadership requires that leadership studies create a paradigm shift in the minds of young men and women, which are plagued with notions of success that focus on wealth, prestige, and status. That, too, is the oxymoronic problem that faces educators, because higher education and success are framed in social status symbols. Discussions must include more important values about why one wants to lead, and the answer should reflect on how organizations choose future leaders.

[40.] Larry W. Boone and Sanya Makhani, "Five Necessary Attitudes of a Servant Leader," *Review of Business* 33, no. 1 (Winter 2012): 87.

[41.] Boone and Makhani, 89.

[42.] Boone and Makhani, 90.

[43.] Boone and Makhani, 92.

[44.] Boone and Makhani, 93.

Leadership is about influence, and as we summarize the potent concept of servant leader, church leaders must realize that any power that exists in the ministry is from God for the specific purpose of fulfilling God's will in building his kingdom. What kinds of things are related to concepts of power in the church? Most scriptural references to "power" are about God's power. However, the church—that is, God's ministers and saints—has "power to witness" (Acts 1:8), power against unclean spirits and to heal the sick (Matthew 10:1), power to tread on serpents and scorpions and over all the power of the enemy (Luke 10:19), power to become the sons of God (John 1:12), power to do miracles (Acts 6:8), and power to give the Holy Spirit (Acts 8:19). These are but a few ways that men of God (and saints) have power within the church. However, leaders within the church must truly understand, "Power without love is destructive."

CHAPTER 9

Leadership Development

The study of leadership is a multidisciplinary field covering topics of styles, traits, structures, behaviors, and functions. Whether concerned with the leader's values, character, or skills, leadership development should be a priority to organizations that expect to expand or survive in a twenty-first-century global marketplace. The making of a leader begins with the choice of a leader, and leadership is about relationship. Effectiveness in leadership must be measured in terms of the quality of the relationship. What are the unique characteristics of the discipleship methods used by Jesus Christ in establishing a worldwide organization—the church? Jesus's leadership development focused on commitment and loyalty rather than scholarship as minimum requirements for leadership. Lack of commitment is now a social illness that has implications for how relationships and thus leadership develop.

Leadership development programs have become important elements of corporate life, but a metaanalysis by Collins and Holton (2004) of eighty-three leadership development programs from 1982 to 2001 revealed, "Overall, the effectiveness of managerial leadership development programs varied widely; some programs were tremendously effective, and others failed miserably.[45]" Acknowledged limitations of the study included a focus only on the business environment, small sample sizes, study design, and, importantly, the relatively few empirical studies at that time available on new intervention methods. The report acknowledges that the lack of studies on leadership interventions is in itself an indication of the difficulty of understanding what it takes to make a leader.

Collins and Holton note that organizations have difficulty in reporting the results of a leadership program because the requirements for leadership are complex and overlapping. The report observes,

> A full range of leadership development experiences includes mentoring, job assignments, feedback systems, on-the-job experiences, developmental relationships, exposure to senior executives, leader-follower relationships, and formal training. While the variety of tasks and challenges encountered on the job are a major source of learning, the reality is that all jobs are not developmentally equal (McCauley and Brutus, 1998), nor can they be expressed in an objective manner, which makes evaluation more difficult.[46]

The obvious challenge presented by understanding the complexities of leadership is that a week, a month, or even a year of leadership training is not sufficient to prepare a leader for any eventuality presented in the leadership role. Task- and knowledge-based expertise can be easily measured, behaviors and personalities examined, and core principles evaluated, but these inputs and outputs of a leadership program do not clearly define a leader. The effectiveness of leadership should be measured by the most critical element—the strength of relationships as they apply to the leader. These include

---

[45.] Doris B. Collins and Ellwood F. Holton, "The Effectiveness of Managerial Leadership Development Programs: A Meta-Analysis of Studies from 1982 to 2001," *Human Resource Development Quarterly* 15, no. 2 (2004): 232.

[46.] Collins and Holton, 232.

leader-leader relationships, leader-follower relationships, and leader-organization relationships.

It is repetitious to mention the debate that has become the founding concern in all leadership studies. Are leaders born or made? Davis writes, "While there may be differing views on what makes a leader, there appears to be consensus in all schools of leadership about this one fact: Leadership is about relationship. Leadership does not exist without someone to lead and someone to follow."[47] Relationship development is fundamental to the understanding of leadership development.

Interestingly both leaders and followers often share common characteristics in terms of expertise, personality, and skill. What makes a leader does not a leader make. No one knew this better than Jesus Christ, who developed the most rigid and restrictive leadership program, which he has since used to create a worldwide organization—the church. Jesus's leadership program began with a calling, then one was chosen for discipleship, and then leadership could only be exercised in the realm of faithfulness. In terms of process, the Bible states, "For many are called, but few are chosen" (Matthew 22:14, KJV), and the end evaluation reads, "And they that are with him are called, chosen, and faithful" (Revelation 17:14, KJV).

The Power of Position

There is always trouble when leadership develops an "us or them" mentality. This is the kind of thinking that grew into a hierarchical structure as the church went from a collegial eldership structure to one where "us" and "them" became known as the "clergy and laity." Frank Damazio writes,

> In their application to the Church of Jesus Christ, the terms "clergy" and "laity" contain seeds both of

---

[47.] Hartwell T. Paul Davis, "Reframing Leadership," Book Review of Lee Bolman and Terrance Deal, Reframing Leadership, in *Business Leadership, edited by Joan Gallos* (San Francisco: Jossey-Bass, 2009), 3. (Liberty University: An Essay Presented in Graduate Studies).

truth and falsehood. It is true that the New Testament presents two general distinctions of ministry. But in doing so, the New Testament never uses the words "clergy" and "laity" or their root meanings.[48]

What is interesting is that the term *clergy*, while applied to ordained church leadership, actually comes from the Old English word meaning "clerk." The word *clerk* was derived from the Latin *clericus*, which really meant a person who was a scholar in a religious order. But Jesus did not put scholarship before character. Nor did Jesus establish a "clergy" position to rule over the church body.

In reality, positional power in which power is defined by the position or office is not the same as leadership. Positional power is what fosters the "us" and "them" mentality within the minds of those subject to it. It does not in itself provide confidence, trust, or respect—all of which are needed by leaders. There is no doubt leverage for getting things done or effecting management efficiency, and the best use of positional power is in management, not leadership. Michael Sales recognizes that positional power exists in most organizations, and the "us and thems" are evident. The four fundamental actors in organizational systems are the tops, bottoms, middles, and environmental players, according to Sales.[49] But what Sales also points out is that in each of these are subsystems also made up of tops, bottoms, and middles. This suggests that leadership is something that permeates throughout an organization at all levels and is not the private domain of a few folks in positions of authority. The challenge for organizations to become robust and dynamic is to balance the elements of differentiation, homogenization, integration, and individuation among members of the organization. This challenge to leadership then is to define relationships not as "us and them" but rather as "we"—partners and members of one another. "Partnership is at the heart of robust systems,"

48. Frank Damazio, *The Making of a Leader* (Portland, OR: City Bible Publishing, 1988), 3.
49. Michael J. Sales, "Leadership and the Power of Position," in Joan V. Gallos (ed.), *Business Leadership* (San Francisco: Jossey-Bass, 2008), 180–198.

according to Sales.[50] That is the concept that Jesus really had in mind when he established the church. It is not an up-and-down, vertical relationship between leaders and followers but rather a horizontal relationship. The vertical axis of the relationship is all members under one head, Jesus Christ. The horizontal axis of the relationship means that all the rest—from leaders to followers—are equal in status. Leadership in this context is not a position but simply a gift of skills to be used to the benefit of the whole organization. This concept is supported by Romans 12, where the "gift" to rule is included with other gifts within the body (Romans 12:6–8, KJV).

This differs to some degree in business, but the concept of being partners and members is a part of recognizing the four basic elements of what people are all about in the robust organization.[51] Differentiation says that people are different, and leaders accept differences in people rather than using them as reasons to create more "them" stereotypes. Everyone is treated fairly and with dignity, without respect to their differences. Homogenization refers to commonality. Everyone, including leaders and followers, are alike in their humanness. All of us have feelings, wants, and needs. This is true of each of us, and the leaders must see how "we" are bound together by the common need to be loved and cared for.

Integration means that "we" all share in a mission, vision, purpose, and direction. There are no fringe elements that cause some to be classified as "thems." Any organization is only as strong as its weakest link. However, individuation was true even among the disciples. Peter was fiery, while John was caring. Thomas was a doubter. James was a disciple of influence. Like in the body, the differences among the members contributed to their own "position power." Paul wrote, "Nay, much more those members of the body, which seem to be more feeble, are necessary" (1 Corinthians 12:22, KJV).

[50.] Sales, 194.

[51.] Sales, 191.

Who Can Be a Leader?

It is not difficult to discover leadership potential. We may not want to give any credibility to a gang leader's ability, but it is there. If we were looking for examples of powerful leadership, our sensitivities may reject Adolph Hitler, Osama bin Laden, or Mao Tse-tung, but they were leaders of influence among millions of followers. It is preferable to use examples of leaders like Steve Jobs of Apple, Bill Gates of Microsoft, or Jack Welsh of General Electric—leaders in the world of business. Historical events have produced a long list of notables, such as Lincoln, Patton, Churchill, Gandhi, and Mandela, as leaders in world affairs. Every organization in order to exist must have a leadership structure.

But leadership is not limited to great men and to those that rise to positions of power, prestige, and notoriety. Leadership always begins with being called and chosen for the role and for the position of leadership. Leadership roles exist at multiple levels throughout organizations, creating levels of leadership, levels of influence, and levels of power. Leaders are chosen from above or from below, by leaders or by followers. The criteria for the choice are usually established by the ones who are choosing the leader. It must be assumed that there are minimum requirements for leadership common to the definition of *leader*, rather than associated with the level of leadership or power structure. With Jesus Christ, the minimum for the lowest rung of leadership is the same for the highest level—and this was demonstrated in the call to discipleship that became a part of the "call to service" required of all that lead in the kingdom of God.

First Principles: Commitment

While leadership programs are for leaders in training or leaders who serve, a discussion of how leaders are chosen is appropriate in whether leadership development programs are effective. The difficulty in determining overall effectiveness of a leadership program is caused by the fact that it is hard to judge how far "the needle should move" in terms of measuring gains from a week-, a month-, or even a yearlong program. However, the intrinsic value of the program might be measured in the amount of time given to building the most important element of leadership—relationship—into the most important form of relationship, one with commitment. If leaders have increased their commitment to the organization and to one another, the program certainly has achieved one aspect of effectiveness.

In modern society, commitment is at an all-time low as evidenced by the rate of divorce in marriage, instability in other relationships, the incessant desire to "chase the dollar," or a culture of self-gratification. Colson and Larson (2010) noted a consensus among recent presidential candidates when asked about changes in young people going to college. They write, "All the candidates said that young adults today are far less willing to commit to anything."[52]

Lack of commitment on the job was revealed in a 2008 study where "more than half of people ages 20 to 24 had been with their current employer for less than a year."[53] It is also reflected in the drop-off in church attendance. Even more shocking are statistics revealed in an evangelism course by Wheeler (2010) from Liberty University, who states, "The US population has increased by 11.4% in the last 10 years while the combined church membership has declined 9.5%." Wheeler notes, "Over half of all churches in the U.S. do not add 1 new church member by conversion. Most add growth by transfers in from other churches.[54]" Growth by transfer reflects a growing lack of commitment to local churches and is a sign of a new social illness that can be found in marriage, religion, and business.

Tenuous relationships have become the norm and predicated on self-interest measured in terms of "satisfaction." Commitment and loyalty are becoming increasingly difficult to find as a part of relationship building, having been replaced by postnuptial agreements in marriage or temporary hiring practices in business. The message is

---

[52] Charles Colson and Catherine Larson, "The Lost Art of Commitment," *Christianity Today* 54, 8 (2010): p. 49.

[53] Colson and Larson, 49.

[54] David Wheeler, "Introduction to Servant Evangelism," a Graduate Course at Liberty University (January 2010).

clear—this relationship depends on many factors, the least of which is commitment.

The necessity of commitment in a relationship represents a core value in the leadership development program established by Jesus Christ—known as discipleship. The meaning of commitment as exemplified in discipleship is found in understanding a relationship where nurturing exists, where dependency is established, and where there are no divided loyalties. These have implications for creating strong leadership relationships as they are important elements of commitment.

Faithfulness in the Face of Failure

Jack Zenger and Joseph Folkman reviewed the results of two studies of more than eleven thousand leaders and identified ten fatal flaws that derail leaders.[55] They compared the results of fired leaders with ineffective leaders and concluded that the ten most common shortcomings in leadership are the following:

- Lacking energy and enthusiasm
- Accepting mediocre performance
- Lacking clear direction and vision
- Having poor judgment
- Lack of collaboration with others
- Do not "walk the talk"
- Resist new ideas
- Do not learn from mistakes
- Lack interpersonal skills
- Failure to develop others

[55.] Jack Zenger and Joseph Folkman, "Ten Fatal Flaws That Derail Leaders," *Harvard Business Review* 87, 6 (June 2009), 18. Retrieved July 20, 2009, from Business Source Complete.

Each of these flaws in leadership can be equated with spiritual deficiencies for which the Bible offers curative suggestions. For example, the Lord created a Sabbath day of rest knowing the physical and spiritual needs of man must both be attended to on a day given to communion with God for restoration. The Lord offers wisdom for those with poor judgment. We read in scripture, "If any of you lack wisdom, let him ask of God, that giveth to all men liberally, and upbraideth not; and it shall be given him" (James 1:5, KJV). Every deficiency has an answer, but in order to keep from failing, the leader must become aware of them. Milliman and Ferguson write, "These sound like obvious flaws that any leader would try to fix. But the ineffective leaders we studied were often unaware that they exhibited these behaviors"[56] (2008, p. 18).

However, great leaders are not those that have never failed or suffered with personal deficiency; great leaders are those who overcame by faithfully using the strengths they had while working on the flaws. They most often sought the spiritual resources of God or others to receive spiritual nourishment in order to tackle their failings. Many leaders use the path of prayer, almost all successful leaders take instruction from mentors or self-help books, and some use other spiritual techniques—whether it is a sabbatical or times of meditation. The most important factor is that all leaders who succeed have "faith in the face of failure." Their faith is evident in their conduct of faithfulness, which simply says, "I will not give up!"

Jim Sullivan readily admits that his failings included several of the ten fatal flaws mentioned by Zenger and Folkman.[57] His failure list included ignoring the advice of others, not recognizing top tal-

---

[56.] John Milliman and Jeffrey Ferguson, "In Search of the 'Spiritual' in Spiritual Leadership: A Case Study of Entrepreneur Steve Bigari," *Business Renaissance Quarterly* 3, no. 1 (Spring 2008): 19–40, http://ezproxy.liberty.edu/login?url=https://search-proquest-com.ezproxy.liberty.edu/docview/212540603?accountid=12085.

[57.] Zenger and Folkman, 18.

ent, and partnering with dishonest people.[58] But Sullivan observes a point that should be well remembered: "Experience teaches only the teachable" (p. 14). Sullivan quotes an old Asian proverb: "Fall down seven times, but stand up eight." Sullivan might have recognized that this was also written by Solomon: "For a just man falleth seven times, and riseth up again" (Proverbs 24:16, KJV).

It is just such a promise that sustained David in the time of his greatest failure. He is best remembered for the one big failure of his life in the matter of Bathsheba, but David's ability to pick himself up after such a long fall was surely because he had learned through many smaller experiences the value of relying on God. David writes, "The steps of a good man are ordered by the Lord: and he delighteth in his way. Though he fall he shall not be utterly cast down: for the Lord upholdeth him with his hand" (Psalm 37:23–24, KJV).

Anticipate and Meet Challenges

"Michael Sales reminds business leaders that organizations are multifaceted social systems that take on a life of their own—and that system dynamics influence individual behavior more than leaders realize."[59] A reminder—leadership is about influence and relationship. The leadership role is fraught with dynamics within the system that is not experienced by others in the relationship. For one, leaders are often the visible symbol of what an organization is all about. Susan Cramm observes, "You're not paranoid. Everyone is watching you." She then observes, "There is power in all the attention—if you use it wisely"[60] (2007, p. 32).

---

58. James Sullivan, "Studying Mistakes with Humility, Discipline Reveals the Lessons That Make Great Leaders," *Nation's Restaurant News* 43, 21 (2009): 14–50. Retrieved July 20, 2009, from Business Source Complete.

59. Joan V. Gallos, *Business Leadership* (San Francisco: Jossey-Bass, 2008), 156.

60. Susan Cramm, "When You're a Leader, Everyone Is Watching You," *CIO* 21, 6 (2007), pp. 32–34. Retrieved July 17, 2009, EBSCOhost, doi:Susanpass:[^] Cramm.

Handling the power of leadership is one of the major challenges for those "who have arrived." Just as power without love is destruction, power without character is destructive. The character of wisdom, love, patience, humility, gentleness, kindness, and long-suffering (elements of the fruit of the spirit) must be present in a leader to prevent corruption and destructive behavior. Hugh Rawson quotes one of the most famous comments on the subject by Lord Acton: "Power tends to corrupt, and absolute power corrupts absolutely."[61] Recent news events are full of scandals in government, including the use of power and influence to manipulate senate seats—as in the Illinois governor's office. American citizens are sick of hearing about earmarks, influence peddling, and the backroom politics in Washington. A Gallup poll in 2008 gave Congress an approval rating of only 14 percent, the lowest since 1992.[62]

Sales writes, "Effective leadership requires more of us: looking below the surface of everyday events, understanding the impact of system dynamics on individual behavior, and learning to leverage the power and possibility of organizational role and position."[63] This means the effective leader needs to understand more about the relationships inherent with the position of leadership and how the leadership position affects the behavior of others.

Making It Happen: The Faithful Leader

In the end, elevation comes when the called and chosen leader remains faithful to the vision received at the calling. According to Andre Delbecq, "Mission, vision, and purpose are brought to life by

---

[61] Hugh Rawson, "Some Rules Aren't Made to Be Broken," In *The Daily Telegraph* (August 26, 2008): Features, 16. Retrieved July 18, 2009, https://www.telegraph.co.uk/news/features/3637804/Some-rules-arent-made-to-be-broken.html.

[62] Lydia Saad, "Congressional Approval Hits Record Low 14%," *Gallup Poll Briefing* (July 16, 2008): 1. Retrieved July 18, 2009, from Business Source Complete: Liberty University.

[63] Michael Sales, 180.

the sense of calling that organizational leaders possess."[64] The calling of a leader becomes the source of the vision, and all of this happens inside the heart and mind of the leader. This is spiritual leadership that is spiritually inspired, and it must be spiritually maintained.

It is the heart and soul of a leader that determine the values and character that ultimately determine the culture of any organization. Milliman and Ferguson see spiritual leadership as "the values, attitudes, and behaviors necessary to intrinsically motivate one's self and others so that they have a sense of spiritual survival through calling and membership."[65] Because the leader's values play such an important part in the overall organizational culture, any failure in leadership has a corresponding negative effect upon the organization. Delbecq points out, "We also know that better than half the strategic decisions made fail because of a leader's human weakness."[66] Within a business or any organization, the principles of spiritual warfare are at work, and this includes a great truth from scripture: "Smite the shepherd and the sheep shall be scattered" (Zechariah 13:7, KJV).

Nourishing the Soul of the Leader

Andre Delbecq makes a powerful observation: "When the outer environment is complex, it becomes critical that the inner remain centered and balanced."[67] While Delbecq contends that the "litmus test of authentic spirituality in all traditions is attention to those in need,"[68] it is important that the leader includes himself in the list. Jesus was known for his prayer life, oftentimes praying all night (Luke 6:12, KJV). He did this not only to nourish his own soul but as an example to his disciples. At one point, Jesus instructed his disci-

---

[64.] Andre Delbecq, "Nourishing the Soul of the Leader," *Business Leadership*, ed. J. V. Gallos (San Francisco: Jossey-Bass, 2008).

[65.] Milliman and Ferguson, 19.

[66.] Delbecq, 493.

[67.] Andre Delbecq, "Nourishing the Soul of the Leader," *Business Leadership*, ed. J. V. Gallos (San Francisco: Jossey-Bass, 2008), 497.

[68.] Delbecq, 500.

ples, "Come ye yourselves apart into a desert place, and rest a while" (Mark 6:31, KJV). There are many instructions throughout the New Testament that speak to reviving our souls, fighting spiritual warfare, obtaining peace, the necessity of prayer, and staying faithful. Many leaders have even learned the value of applying Christian principles to guiding their own spirituality in the secular workplace.

Leadership development is a process. Leadership theories have looked at behavior, character, and personality. Studies of leadership have focused on charisma, spirituality, motivation, introversion, extroversion, and all possibilities to define leadership, many times with the hope that doing so will help organizations make the right leadership choices. In the end, the process is the same on earth as it is in heaven; it is a matter of being one of the called, chosen, and faithful. Leadership more than anything is about the heart of the leader, and it was Talleyrand who summed up leadership from the eyes of those being led: "I am more afraid of an army of 100 sheep led by a lion than an army of 100 lions led by a sheep."[69]

[69.] Stephen P. Robbins and Timothy A. Judge, *Organizational Behavior*, 13th ed. (Upper Saddle River, NJ: Prentice Hall, 2009), 382.

CHAPTER 10

The Called, Chosen, and Faithful Leader

Leaders are made, not born. Like so many other complex life issues, the question of nature versus nurture in leadership is one that is analyzed, researched, and debated by educators, philosophers, social scientists, and even leaders themselves. Leadership has been dissected as to personality, character, and behavior. Researchers have developed tests, established programs, and created the best graduate-level courses to study, train, and develop leaders. While there may be differing views on what makes a leader, there appears to be consensus in all schools of leadership about one fact of leadership: leadership is about relationship. Leadership does not exist without someone to lead and someone to follow.

What is leadership? John Maxwell quotes J. Oswald Sanders, which states simply, "Leadership is influence."[70] Robbins and Judge expand the definition and write, "We define leadership as the ability to influence a group toward the achievement of a vision or set of goals."[71] While leaders typically "have authority" and "do management," Bolman and Deal state that leadership is distinct from

---

[70.] John C. Maxwell and Tim Elmore, "Leadership Is Influence," Section: God Has Already Called You to Lead, *The Maxwell Leadership Bible*, 2nd ed. (Nashville, TN: Thomas Nelson, 2007).

[71.] Robbins and Judge, 385.

authority and different from management. Bolman and Deal observe in *Reframing Organizations* that leadership is not something that is tangible but something that exists only in relationships. It is in the perception of the engaged parties.[72]

Since leadership is about relationship, we must look then to the development of relationship from which the roles of leader and follower emerge. There can be no better example of the making of leaders than in looking at Jesus and his disciples. While some leaders change companies, and a few have changed nations, Jesus developed leaders that changed the world.

Jesus, the Master Symbolic Leader

If leaders are made and not born, the question must be asked, how are they made, and who makes them? In the narrowest sense, a leader can be made by any foolish person that chooses to not think for themselves and simply follows the influence of someone else, whether it is right or wrong. Jesus speaks to this kind of relationship when he speaks of "blind leaders of the blind" (Matt. 15:14, KJV). Unfortunately there are those that are self-appointed leaders that use force or persuasion to gain power and to keep power. Such was the case of a man called Diotrephes, who according to John "loved to have the preeminence" (3 John 1:9, KJV). Then you have those that are appointed by men to positional power, as happens in political patronage; or born into positional power, as in the case of royalty. But these are not real leaders that will produce meaningful results. Usually some catastrophe or negative consequence will result that brings down the leader. It is not to say that some leaders don't emerge out of such circumstances, but actual leadership develops in spite of how a person got there, not because of patronage or royalty.

Real leaders are produced by relationship, transformed by relationship, and are sustained by relationship, and most always it is the

---

[72.] Lee G. Bolman and Terrence E. Deal, "Reframing Leadership," in J. V. Gallos (ed.), *Business Leadership* (San Francisco: Jossey-Bass, 2008), 35.

product of mentoring by other leaders. Gabriella Salvatore echoes the mantra that leaders are developed, not born, and contends that no one is better qualified to teach leadership skills than leaders themselves.[73] The foundations of leadership, according to Salvatore, include four relationship management competencies: communication, coaching, influence, and managing for change. Salvatore shares some of the formal knowledge transfer practices of the mentor, including coaching, stretch assignments, job shadowing, and video libraries of "war stories." These align well with the practices and rules of symbolic leadership suggested by Bolman and Deal, which are the following:

- Lead by example: Salvatore's job shadowing
- Use symbols to capture attention: a part of coaching
- Frame experience—what experience is gained on those "stretch assignments"?
- Communicate a vision
- Tell stories[74]

It isn't always a video library, but this is an important part of mentoring. To reiterate a review of the article by Bolman and Deal, Jesus was the master of the five practices of symbolic leadership:

- Jesus led by example. He made disciples of men.
- Jesus used symbols to capture attention. These were his miracles.
- Symbolic leaders frame experience. Jesus spoke to everyday issues using everyday examples. Each day was a new day of learning for his disciples because they followed Jesus and experienced what he experienced.
- Symbolic leaders communicate a vision. His message was eternal life and a heavenly kingdom. He prepared his disciples for service.
- Symbolic leaders tell stories. These were his parables.

---

73. Gabriella Salvatore, "Develop Tomorrow's Leaders," *Training* 46, 5 (June 2009): 38. Retrieved July 13, 2009, from Business Source Complete: Liberty University.

74. Bolman and Deal, 35–49.

The Vision of Leadership

Leadership is a product of relationship. In order to be a leader, one must have followers; otherwise a person might simply be a manager. Robbins and Judge state, "Management consists of implementing the vision and strategy provided by leaders…"[75] There will always be the need for leaders to develop managers. But one of the great purposes of leadership is the development of successors. Leadership development is a core strategy of succession planning. Leaders with vision do not limit their vision to one solitary life. John Maxwell lists twenty-one qualities of great leaders. One of those qualities is the quality of vision. Maxwell shares "Lessons from Abraham on Vision" and writes that a vision must "be bigger than the leader" (Notes, Gen. 17:1–8, KJV). Maxwell writes, "While Abraham wanted to father an heir, God wanted him to father nations."[76] Vision is a part of the calling of leadership.

Aligning with the Vision

Leadership development for the church is a process that operates in the framework of discipleship mandated by the final words of Jesus Christ before ascending into heaven. Huizing (2011) observes, "Discipleship, then, appears to be the primary initiative not only in increasing the number of followers of Jesus but also in the development of Christ-following leaders."[77]

The relationship between a leader candidate and the vision must first be determined before entering a school of leadership. If leadership initiatives seem to yield weak results, it requires an examination of vision alignment, including the commitment elicited from what are core principles associated with the vision.

[75.] Robbins and Judge, 385.

[76.] John C. Maxwell and Tim Elmore, "On 21 Qualities, Notes on Genesis 12:1–22:4," *The Maxwell Leadership Bible*, 2nd ed. (Nashville, TN: Thomas Nelson, 2007).

[77.] Russell L. Huizing, "Leaders from Disciples: The Church's Contribution to Leadership Development," *Evangelical Review of Theology* 35, 4 (2011): 4.

CHAPTER 11

The Called Leader

Davis posits that leadership is a result of a "calling." The metaphor implies the development of a relationship between one that is called and that who calls. In his essay, "The Called, Chosen, and Faithful Leader," Davis writes,

> There are two types of calling in the making of leaders. One is a special calling to a first in line leader. This first calling either comes from God or the calling comes from purpose, as related to human events. This is where the initial vision is received, the first inspiration, the beginning of a line of leadership. Examples of the first calling included Abraham, Moses, David, Jesus, Mohammad, Gandhi, Ford, Edison, and the list goes on.[78]

Callings that result from human events are those that are not based upon a prior relationship, but the event defines the call to leadership. It is likely that even these examples are the handiwork of God.

[78.] Hartwell T. P. Davis, "The Called, Chosen, and Faithful Leader," *Education Resources Information Center*, ED506263 (2009). Retrieved from http://www.eric.ed.gov/ERICWebPortal/search/permalinkPopup.jsp?accno=ED506263.

Daniel declares that it is God who sets up kings and removes kings; therefore, all leaders are under the rule of God even though they may not know it (Daniel 2:20–21, KJV).

The first type of calling is exemplified by leaders such as Lincoln, Churchill, and Mandela, who receive their vision from the event that marks their life and transforms their leadership into that which defines them. Oftentimes this second calling does not signify the beginning of an organization or nation, but it may signify the beginning of a vision intended for mankind. Lincoln's vision of freedom from slavery, Churchill's vision for world peace, and Mandela's vision of the eradication of apartheid are not without significance.

The importance of vision as "the calling" is that it defines the purpose of the leader, the purpose of the call, and the purpose of the organization being led. The call creates a relationship, a bond, between the call and the one called. All other relationships are judged in relation to the share of vision for which they become responsible. The vision of Jesus Christ was a worldwide church that would exist for eternity, that would represent the kingdom of God on earth until the end of human history, and that would have a primary mission, which was summarized in what has become known as the Great Commission: "Go ye therefore and teach all nations, baptizing them in the name of the Father, the Son, and the Holy Ghost, teaching them to observe all things whatsoever I have commanded you" (Matthew 28:19–20, KJV).

In the first calling, whether by God or events, the vision is revealed. In the second, the vision is transferred. That first vision is usually unique to a religious leader, company founder, inventor, church planter, entrepreneur, warrior-leader, or father of a nation. Succeeding leaders get parts or perhaps all of that vision in the rite of succession, and their share of the vision may be modified—grow, change, or even replaced.

The second calling is the calling of succession leaders by leaders to carry on the first leader's vision. Great examples of the second calling are Abraham to Isaac, then Isaac to Jacob; Moses to Joshua; David to Solomon; and Jesus to his disciples and Jesus to Paul. In each case, the purpose of the calling was to pass on the first leader's vision. The same is true in the corporate world as leaders are called by other leaders to carry forward the vision of growth, the great ideas, or the life's purpose of the first leader.

It does not matter whether a leader is a first-in-line leader with a vision for a product, service, or organization, or one that receives a vision from human events; leaders must develop followers based on the vision that the leaders possess. In order for leadership to be developed in an organization, all leadership must become subject to the vision of the one that makes the call. The vision must then be considered the root cause of all leadership functions throughout an organization. Otherwise what exist are competing visions representing a "house divided" that cannot stand (Matthew 12:25, KJV).

CHAPTER 12

The Chosen Leader

Jesus declares, "Many are called but few are chosen" (Matthew 22:14, KJV). Sometimes leaders are selected by followers, but most of the time, leaders are selected by leaders. In the Bible, we find examples of both processes, but what is interesting is that the follower-selected leaders actually performed management, while leader-selected leaders became leaders. An example of follower-selected leaders (actually managers) is the selection of deacons in the first church. There was a need to organize and manage the distribution of food and goods to the widows of the church. The gentile women felt they were being neglected (Acts 6:1, KJV). In order to solve the problem, someone was needed to manage the daily ministrations, so the apostles gave these instructions to the people to select leaders from among them (Acts 6:3, KJV). These deacons were selected by their peers, then were appointed by the apostles.

Most leaders in the church and in business are chosen by leaders. While some fundamental churches use the process of congregational vote to select pastors, the process is far from scriptural. The choosing of elders was not in the hands of the congregation but a responsibility of the apostles and elders. Paul and Barnabas were both apostles (Acts 14:14, KJV) who then ordained elders in each of the churches under their ministry (Acts 14:21–23, KJV). We later find Titus ordaining elders in every city on Crete (Titus 1:5, KJV) and Timothy receiving instructions from Paul on the process of ordaining both elders and deacons (1 Timothy 3, KJV). Leadership development in the Bible was leader to leader, not follower to leader. Jesus said, "Ye have not chosen me, but I have chosen you and ordained you..." (John 15:16, KJV). Succession planning is used by church leaders rarely, and as a result, churches are often required to do the best they can in finding a new pastor. Outgoing pastors or organizational church leaders should be responsible for guiding the process of bringing in new leadership into local churches.

The same is true in the business world. This has given rise to the increased growth of leadership development programs in business organizations. Robbins and Judge write, "Organizations, in aggregate, spend billions of dollars, yen, and euros on leadership training and development. These efforts take many forms—from $50,000 executive leadership programs offered by universities such as Harvard to sailing experiences at the Outward-Bound School. Business schools, including some elite programs, such as Dartmouth, MIT, and Stanford, are placing renewed emphasis on leadership development."[79]

Robbins and Judge, however, make an interesting observation: "First let us recognize the obvious. People are not equally trainable."[80] This conclusion means that choosing a leader means more than looking at the academics of leadership development courses and classroom-earned credentials. Sally Kalin observes that many leadership programs turn out administrators rather than leaders. Some programs, however, such as the Harvard Leadership Institute, goes beyond most others by forcing participants "to examine their own leadership styles through a path of self-discovery covering three themes: how you lead, what you lead, and where you lead from."[81]

There are great programs that have turned out great leaders, and to some degree, these are modeled after the strictest leadership development program ever imagined. The leadership program of Jesus is

---

[79.] Stephen P. Robbins and Timothy A. Judge, *Organizational Behavior*, 13th ed. (Upper Saddle River, NJ: Prentice Hall, 2009), 436.

[80.] Robbins and Judge, 436.

[81.] Sally W. Kalin, "Reframing Leadership: The Acrl/Harvard Leadership Institute for Academic Librarians," *Journal of Business & Finance Librarianship* 13, no. 3 (2008): 261–70.

a model for leaders that hope to bring about great change. This program required meeting the tests of discipleship, which required operating in the realm of faith, and also the development of character.

Discipleship Development

Being chosen for Jesus's leadership development program required the disciples to make the most extraordinary commitment—everything they possessed. Chosen leaders are committed leaders. Consider the minimum requirement for the Lord's disciples:

> If any man come to me, and hate not his father, and mother, and wife, and children, and brethren, and sisters, yea, and his own life also, he cannot be my disciple. And whosoever doth not bear his cross, and come after me, cannot be my disciple. (Luke 14:26–27, KJV)

Throughout the discipleship process, Jesus constantly addressed the priorities required to be great leaders. While the text uses language that might be misunderstood by some, the disciples understood the principle that commitment to Jesus Christ, to a mission, to a vision means that these become first in their hearts and minds. Even the idea of success and wealth was not a concept of the Lord's school of leadership. Jesus said, "Ye cannot serve God and mammon [money]" (Matthew 6:24, KJV). The emphasis on wealth in many business school programs is detrimental in developing true leaders.

Unfortunately many business schools today emphasize personal reward rather than personal sacrifice. Joel Padony, in writing for the *Harvard Business Review*, comments, "Unless America's business schools make radical changes, society will become convinced that MBAs work to serve only their self-interest."[82] Padony contrasts business schools from schools that are really turning out professionals and great leaders by looking at what needs to be emphasized. Followers do not trust leaders when they believe the leader's motive is more about money and self-interest than the interest of the followers. Padony suggests,

> In order to reduce people's distrust, business schools need to show that they value what society values. They need to teach the principles, ethics, and attention to detail that are the essential components of leadership, and they need to place a greater emphasis on leadership's responsibilities—not just its rewards.[83]

Chosen leaders must be committed to the vision, not the rewards, and Jesus only chose one "thief" for his purposes (John 12:6, KJV). He did not choose Judas for leadership. Commitment will always be one of the first qualities looked for in leadership. Because Jesus knew that the ultimate sacrifice was to be paid by those he chose, he required the ultimate commitment.

Trichinotis and Scheiner contend that commitment is a part of the ultimate mission of a leader, and write,

> The ultimate mission of the committed leader is not found in personal gold medals. Rather it is rooted in a personal commitment based on one simple philosophy: "Service before self." "Service before self" (better known as the second Air Force core value) is more plainly defined as putting personal agendas aside for the good of the organization and the people within an organization. The element of com-

82. Joel M. Padony, "The Buck Stops and Starts at Business Schools," *Harvard Business Review*, June issue (2009), https://hbr.org/2009/06/the-buck-stops-and-starts-at-business-school.

83. Padony, 64.

mitment is the first and foremost requirement of all leaders that are choosing leaders to succeed them.[84]

The chosen leader must live in the realm of faith. Human nature is to live within the comfort zone of experience and tradition. This includes the path of least resistance in what we choose to believe or decisions that we make. Attributed to Francis Bacon is this observation: "Man prefers to believe what he prefers to be true." In other words, our minds, thoughts, and beliefs are constrained by what Steven Sample calls our "binary thinking."[85] These are the yes or no, true or false, right or wrong, and good or bad kinds of thinking. One that every leader contends with is the "can or can't" thinking that happens in the decision-making process. Binary thinking is easy, quick, and much less work than really having to process data from many sources and find answers in ways never experienced before.

Binary thinking is the norm; "most people are binary and instant in their judgments."[86] It is thinking that is constrained by the tendency to "believe the last thing heard" (p. 117), be influenced by the congenital naysayers (p. 119), and think in well-worn ruts (p. 124).[87] It is the kind of thinking that is fraught with skepticism, which is a condition that borders on unbelief. The definition of *skepticism* includes "systematic doubt" (*Merriam-Webster Online*).

A part of the leadership development program of Jesus was to constantly challenge the disciples to live in the realm of faith—the ability to think outside the box. Jesus used miracles to grow the faith of the disciples. Because Jesus was to later "endue them with power from on high," he must first walk them through the experiences of miracles, where overcoming doubt and the constraints of the natural senses could be accomplished. We know of only one early learner,

---

[84] M. Trichinotis and G. Scheiner, "Committed Leadership: Going for the Gold," *Armed Forces Comptroller* 41, no. 4 (1996): 39. Retrieved July 15, 2009, from Business Source Complete.

[85] Steven B. Sample, "Thinking Gray and Free," in Joan V. Gallos (ed.), *Business Leadership* (San Francisco: Jossey-Bass, 2008), pp. 115–124.

[86] Sample, 115.

[87] Sample, 124.

which was Peter—the only one willing to step out of the boat and walk on water (Matthew 14:22–30, KJV)—and he was the one that eventually received the "keys of the kingdom" (Matt. 16:19, KJV).

Chosen leaders are those that have proven they have ability for creative thinking, can make tough decisions that are contrary to conventional wisdom, and, most importantly, can pass the "challenge testing" of their mentors. The chosen leader must exemplify character over personality. Frank Damazio hits home on this point, particularly in reference to the church leadership of today.

Tragically today's overemphasis on academic degrees has contributed to the pride, hypocrisy, and spiritual lifelessness in many of the church's leaders. As we shall see in the Bible, God does not emphasize the academic development of his leaders as much as their development in character, wisdom, and piety.[88] Even the secular world regards character as the most important quality of a leader. Alan Davis of Massey University writes,

> Like never before our organizations need authentic leadership. Leadership characterized by consistency of character—not text book techniques; visibility to the people affected by their decisions; leadership that understands the power of symbols that demonstrate alignment between what leaders promise and what the organization does.[89]

David Benzel observes in *Shed the Superman Cape*, "Credibility is the key ingredient to leadership."[90] The ability to trust a leader does not come from academic success, personality, or even business

---

88. Frank Damazio, *The Making of a Leader* (Portland, OR: City Bible Publishing, 1988), 2.

89. Alan Davis, "Authentic Leadership: Future Proofing Your Organization's Reputation," *Human Resources Magazine* June/July, 14, 2 (2009): p. 1. Retrieved July 17, 2009, from Business Source Complete: Liberty University.

90. Benzel, David, "Build Credibility: Shed the Superman Cape," *Leadership Excellence* 25, 1 (2008): pp. 12–14. Retrieved July 2, 2009, from Business Source Complete database: Liberty University.

achievement; it comes from authenticity and integrity. Damazio defines character as "the sum total of all the negative and positive qualities in a person's life, exemplified by one's thoughts, values, motivations, attitudes, feelings and actions."[91] Notice that this definition begins with what are the internals of a person and ends with actions.

Character becomes the most noticeable part of leadership. Stephen Long quotes Admiral David Zumwalt, who calls such character "executive presence," saying, "Executive presence arises from a multifaceted set of skills. The leader must exude authenticity, which includes confidence, competence, and the ability to engage emotionally, as well." Zumwalt further comments, "Executive presence combines the heart and mind of the leader."[92] All of this means simply that character shows.

This is the reason why specific requirements for eldership were outlined in the Bible. These did not include credentials, talent, personality, speaking ability, or pedigree. Instead requirements included being above reproach, blameless, not greedy, patient, and more (1 Timothy 3:1–7, KJV). It was all about character on the inside that could be seen on the outside.

---

91. Damazio, 106.
92. Long, Stephen, "Executive Presence: What Is It and How to Get It," *Nonprofit World* 29, no. 6 (2011): 14–15.

CHAPTER 13

The Faithful Leader

The Greek word *mathetas*, which is translated "disciple," is frequently used in the New Testament for followers of John the Baptist and followers of Jesus Christ. The meaning of the noun *disciple* is "one who is a pupil; a learner." The root word *manthano* means "to learn," but conceptually it has been used for one who is an understudy or apprentice. Herrick (n.d.) expounds on the term, noting that culturally, it goes beyond that of being a mere student. Herrick writes, "The Sophists also used the term to refer to an 'institutional pupil.'"[93] However, the mere meaning of the word *disciple* as a pupil does injustice to a concept that would now simply refer to one that goes to school. Discipleship in the biblical context and as required by Jesus took precedence over all natural relationships, requiring that one become fully committed both physically and spiritually to one teacher and one vision. The commitment brought with it the assumption of total dependence for all of one's needs. Harder (1963) posits that Christian education as represented by Jesus's discipleship had three concepts: "Christian nurture, Christian instruction, and Christian experience."

Commitment is part of the process of receiving nurture from relationships, typically from familial relationships. It is the normal

---

[93] Greg Herrick, "Understanding the Meaning of the Term Disciple," *Bible.org*, Series Go Make Disciples of All Nations 2 (2004). Retrieved from https://bible. org/seriespage/2-understanding-meaning-term-disciple.

source of dependency and in most cultures engenders the strongest of emotional ties. Family relationships are the most common source of values, emotional support, and for the young, material support. Interestingly, more than any other relationship, Jesus focused on natural family relationships as the greatest barrier to becoming one of his disciples.

Jesus used difficult language, stating, "If any man come to me, and hate not his father, and mother, and wife, and children, and brethren, and sisters, yea, and his own life also, he cannot be my disciple" (Luke 14:26, KJV). The Greek word *miseo*, translated "hate," has been deemed "love less" by most scholars. In a context where love and marriage refer to becoming "one flesh," Jesus uses terminology that indicates a separation from the natural family, being bound together instead in relationship with Jesus and the new family of disciples. When Jesus is confronted with the presence of his natural family, he quickly rejected all natural relationships. The Bible declares,

> But he answered and said unto him that told him, Who is my mother? and who are my brethren? And he stretched forth his hand toward his disciples, and said, Behold my mother and my brethren! For whosoever shall do the will of my Father which is in heaven, the same is my brother, and sister, and mother. (Matthew 12:48–50)

The significance of the change in relationship is the importance of the changing source of nurture on which a disciple must become totally dependent. Not only are family relationships included in what must be given up, but a disciple must give up dependence on all worldly goods, looking to Jesus as the new source of nurture and fulfillment of all needs. Jesus states,

> There is no man that hath left house, or brethren, or sisters, or father, or mother, or wife, or children, or land for my sake, and the gospels, But he shall receive an hundredfold now in this time,

houses, and brethren, and sisters, and mothers, and children, and lands, with persecutions; and in the world to come eternal life. (Mark 10:29–30)

In the process of discipleship, Jesus reiterated such dependency when he instructed his disciples. The Bible records,

And he called unto him the twelve, and began to send them forth by two and two; and gave them power over unclean spirits; And commanded them that they should take nothing for their journey, save a staff only; no scrip, no bread, no money in their purse: But be shod with sandals; and not put on two coats. (Mark 6:7–9)

The requirements of discipleship were metaphorical in that such phrases as "take up your cross," "hate not his father," or "forsaking his own life" are metaphorical. Jesus did not intend for a disciple to divorce or leave his wife or abandon his children as the price of service. These would have been contrary to scripture, and the Bible is replete with family instruction for Christians and Christian leaders, including the qualifications for elders and deacons. Jesus did not intend for such relationships to be sacrificed on the altar of neglect, but it was in recognizing that worldly relationships have a way of controlling the heart, that a change was required.

In order for leaders to grow in relationships, they must find within an organization a source of nurturing and the expectation that dependency needs will be shared. Commitment is a matter of heart, not contract, and it is in this context that leadership should be exercised. An organization should be viewed as family, where values of closeness, sharing, emotional ties, and support are a part of the cultural experience. Leaders in such organizations take on the roles of caretakers, providers, and protectors. It is no wonder that Paul could write, "For though ye have ten thousand instructors in Christ yet have ye not many fathers: for in Christ Jesus I have begotten you through the gospel" (1 Corinthians 4:15, KJV).

Discipleship: A Test of Loyalty

The test of discipleship meant that a leader must not have divided loyalties. The admonition listing the several things that were to be "hated" can be considered as a reasonable test against ethical dilemmas that will be faced in the life of a leader. Family, wealth, and self can create loyalties that can cloud judgment. The issue is who shall be served, and if this includes favoritism, nepotism, or self-interest, the decision making of a leader suffers.

This explains such scriptures where the natural family is seen as spiritual hindrances to a disciple of Jesus Christ. Jesus says,

> Think not that I am come to send peace on earth: I came not to send peace, but a sword. For I am come to set a man at variance against his father, and the daughter against her mother, and the daughter in law against her mother in law. And a man's foes shall be they of his own household. He that loveth father or mother more than me is not worthy of me: and he that loveth son or daughter more than me is not worthy of me. And he that taketh not his cross, and followeth after me, is not worthy of me. He that findeth his life shall lose it: and he that loseth his life for my sake shall find it. (Matthew 10:34–39)

In the kingdom of God, family traditions and religious ties are among the strongest challenges for the truth seeker and the most common argument for rejecting more truth. Who has not heard, "My mother was Catholic, and I will die a Catholic," or, "My family is Baptist, and no one can tell me differently"? These are natural statements of family loyalty, but in the kingdom of God, family loyalty must always be second to the will of God. It is only by placing God first can a person "walk in the light" (1 John 1:7), either validating or finding what is true.

Just as Christians must often choose between family loyalties and serving God in a different way, leaders must often make decisions that are in the best interest of an organization but that are not in the interest of the organizational family. Leaders must ask the question, "Whose needs are being met?" The answer is where a leader's loyalties lie.

Jesus's discipleship method was designed to measure the first principles for leadership, commitment, and loyalty. Modern leadership programs do not have in place the strong restrictive measures exhibited in biblical discipleship, and developing tests for commitment and loyalty in our modern global society—where mobility abounds—would represent a challenge. The first principles of commitment and loyalty should become constructs of any leadership development program.

CHAPTER 14

Maladaptive Church Leadership

As we can see, the answer to the question, "Are leaders born or made?" is yes! Just as nature and nurture contribute to our being as a person, nature and nurture contribute to personalities, characteristics, and skills that operate in the life of a leader. Like it or not, even physical characteristics can make a difference in the kind of influence one person may have over another. If leadership is a skill that can be developed, for example, opportunity is key for developing skills. Physical appearance can impact one's opportunities in the workplace, and it can also impact perceptions of would-be followers. An article in *Estates Gazette* (2012) notes, "Research by Professors Timothy Judge and Daniel Cable showed that taller employees earn more money on average than shorter employees. Employers are subconsciously short-changing (pardon the pun) some employees because of their height. Could this be an angle for a lateral-thinking lawyer to pursue?" This does not presume that being short will automatically hinder leadership ability. Interestingly, being overweight is a common occurrence among preachers, but while obesity is a common discriminator in the workforce, there are many factors that impact how leadership really develops. For years, the color of the skin or the gender of a person could negatively impact a person's opportunity, which in turn could impact how leadership skills can develop. While lack of opportunity may not impact all the characteristics needed for leadership, it does impact skill development, which is also essential for leadership. However, Paul is said to have been short in stature, but leadership theories, when it comes to the church, do not always hold true.

Truly one of the most overlooked leadership theories is the Lord's discipleship program, which I covered in the discussion in "The Called, Chosen, and Faithful Leader" section of this book. When it comes to the church, many leadership theories can be thrown out of the door. Indeed we do have examples that suggest that height can impact equal opportunity, but in the kingdom of God, God does not look for leaders in the same way that man looks for leaders. Take, for example, the story of David. When God sent Samuel to Jesse's house to anoint one of his sons as the next king of Israel, even in the eyes of Samuel, Eliab, Jesse's oldest son, seemed to be a perfect choice. However, God thought different:

> And it came to pass, when they were come, that he looked on Eliab, and said, Surely the LORD'S anointed is before him. But the LORD said unto Samuel, Look not on his countenance, or on the height of his stature; because I have refused him: for the LORD seeth not as man seeth; for man looketh on the outward appearance, but the LORD looketh on the heart. (1 Samuel 16:6–7, KJV)

It is interesting that the first king, Saul, was head and shoulders above every other man in Israel (1 Samuel 9:1). What must be understood is that God has complete control over whom he calls, and the key to leadership is continuing in the will of God to fulfill God's purposes in the church.

Three Spirits That Damage Church Leadership

The overarching and single most important principle for being a God-called leader is being a "God-called leader." Note the play on words. One of the greatest—and I believe most profound—statements from E. L. Holley, president of Texas Bible College, was when he said, "Whom the Lord calls, God qualifies." Church leaders, referring to elders and deacons in the governmental roles and the fivefold ministry in the servant's role, must have the spiritual anointing and unction that provides the talent gifts needed for whatever service God requires. The parable of the talents indicates that not all gifts are the same and not all results will be the same (Matthew 25:15–28). It is not unusual for church dynasties to develop, and while many of these "successions" are ordained by God, there are those situations where the son of a preacher is not called to be a preacher. Often they are, but as we previously alluded to preacher "wannabes," it is essential that a minister knows the difference between the voice of God and the voice of a grandmother or a father when taking on the mantle of ministry.

Every leader must be aware that there are three major syndromes that damage the ministry more than anything else in the modern church. All three are the result of the maladaptive influences of three spirits that ruin both the leadership ministry and the body ministry of the church. These three maladaptive influences are recorded in Jude 1:11: "Woe unto them! for they have gone in the way of Cain and ran greedily after the error of Balaam for reward and perished in the gainsaying of Core."

The Spirit of Cain

The first spirit that can damage church leadership and church growth is the spirit of "Cain," which is the spirit of jealousy. One statement that has stuck with me through the years was from a fine preacher in Erie, Pennsylvania, who stated in one sermon, "Comparison is the mother of all discontent." The real focus of comparison is not the other person but is a form of self-interest and one of being self-centered. Apostle Paul observed,

> For we dare not make ourselves of the number
> or compare ourselves with some that commend

themselves: but they measuring themselves by themselves, and comparing themselves among themselves, are not wise. But we will not boast of things without *our* measure, but according to the measure of the rule which God hath distributed to us, a measure to reach even unto you. For we stretch not ourselves beyond *our measure*, as though we reached not unto you: for we are come as far as to you also in *preaching* the gospel of Christ: Not boasting of things without *our* measure, *that is*, of other men's labours; but having hope, when your faith is increased, that we shall be enlarged by you according to our rule abundantly, To preach the gospel in the *regions* beyond you, *and* not to boast in another man's line of things made ready to our hand. But he that glorieth, let him glory in the Lord. For not he that commendeth himself is approved, but whom the Lord commendeth. (2 Corinthians 10:12–18, KJV)

Before I went to New York as a home missionary, Pastor Nathaniel Urshan, who at that time was the general superintendent of the United Pentecostal Church, spoke to me, intent on giving me some encouragement. I had been blessed under the ministry of Corlis Dees and a very large church in Houston, Texas, but Pastor Urshan told me, "Paul, a church of fifty in New York is like a church of five hundred in Texas." Knowing that the Northeast United States was not the Bible belt, I was not to get discouraged or disappointed if my planting would not have the same result as that to which I was accustomed. He also let me know, "If a man has the gift of pastoring five hundred, he will take a church of fifty and grow it to five hundred. If his gift is pastoring a church of fifty, he will take a church of five hundred and eventually have a church of fifty." While that can be a horrible thought, the reality is that God knows where to put us, and we must learn to rejoice when others are blessed and trust God for the increase.

The Spirit of Balaam

The second spirit that will destroy ministry, whether individually or in the church body, is the spirit of Balaam, which I shall identify is the "gift for gain" spirit. In the story of Balaam, he was offered honor and riches by Balak, the king of Moab, to curse the Israel as they came out of Egypt. Notice that God had a prophet, Balaam, outside of the nation of Israel, which shows that the knowledge of God is never limited to those who are in the church. This does not have anything to do with the issue of salvation, but it does have something to do with understanding how God reveals himself throughout the world. Balaam was not only God's prophet, but he indicated a sense of original faithfulness in stating, "If Balak would give me his house full of silver and gold, I cannot go beyond the word of the Lord, to do less or more" (Numbers 22:18, KJV). Unfortunately, temptation eventually caused Balaam to falter as he found a way around God's Word to cause Moab to Israel to sin, meaning that Israel brought a curse upon itself (Numbers 31:16). Although the text in Numbers does not tell the whole story of how Balaam gave in to temptation, the apostle Peter reveals that many false prophets have "forsaken the right way, and are gone astray, following the way of Balaam, the son of Bosor, who loved the wages of unrighteousness" (2 Peter 2:15, KJV).

While the Bible does not condemn wealth or having riches, for God often has blessed many of his people with material wealth, it is what is in the heart that can turn blessings into cursing. The proliferation of televangelists and even religious cult leaders, with incomes far beyond the typical livelihood of most ministers in general, can be suspect. This does not mean that all such ministers are using their "gift for gain," for only God can judge the heart. However, the scripture warned,

> But godliness with contentment is great gain. For we brought nothing into *this* world, *and it is* certain we can carry nothing out. And having food and raiment let us be therewith content. But they

that will be rich fall into temptation and a snare, and *into* many foolish and hurtful lusts, which drown men in destruction and perdition. For the love of money is the root of all evil: which while some coveted after, they have erred from the faith, and pierced themselves through with many sorrows. (1 Timothy 6:5–10)

However, gift for gain is not limited to the concept of money. Fame, fortune, personal aggrandizement, and pride are other ways that the spirit of Balaam can exist in the church. For example, when someone prays in Old English, could it be that they are wanting to appear more spiritual? Just saying. Can the gift of tongues or the gift of prophecy be used to bring attention to oneself? It is possible, and God forbid that this happens. Does the gift of healing ever get abused? In the story of Jim Jones, it is recorded that he used one of his church secretaries to disguise herself as an old lady who miraculously was healed from being lame. In my own experience, and I won't name the preacher involved, I have spoken to those who claim that they had been recruited to be foils in healing ministry campaigns. Does it happen? Yes, it does. Is it widespread? I doubt it because the healing gift is real and the number of healings and miracles in the church are beyond being counted.

None of these examples are meant to generalize the gift for gain spirit, and again God will bring judgment on such falsehood, but the reality is that the cancer does exist within the church.

The Spirit of Kore (Korah)

The third spirit that can destroy the ministry of the church is the spirit of rebellion. Whether among church leaders or among the flock, rebellion can be manifested many ways. One of the reasons for this book is to make clear that accountability is an important part of God's plan for leadership. How can ministers of God expect saints to be in a right relationship with God, who has all authority, if rejection of authority is a pattern of life? Attitudes concerning authority, responsibility, and accountability become a part of our value system and our spirit, and these attitudes determine our relationship with those in authority. Whether in the family, school, workplace, or government, authorities exist, and even if a person lives alone on an island or as a hermit in the mountains, we all are subject to the ultimate authority of God, who will eventually judge us in eternity. The judgment for our behaviors will always begin with the judgment of our hearts and attitudes. After all, one scriptural truism by Solomon is "Keep thy heart with all diligence for out it are the issues of life" (Proverbs 4:23, KJV).

How does rebellion manifest itself in leadership? First, if we are independent from ministerial relationship with others, do we know why? Although there are reasons why a minister may not belong to a ministerial organization, that does not mean that fellowship with other ministers should not be a part of our lives. Within the local church, does the pastor have accountability structures? How good are we at taking advice or suggestions from those who are above us, below us, or who are our peers? May I suggest a caution that anyone who thinks that only God can tell him what to do has given in to self-deception. God's Word is full of admonitions that enjoin submission in various ways.

The Peter, Paul, Apollos Syndrome

What is the most likely result to the church leadership or the church body when the aforementioned spirits exist within the church? It is division that manifest itself through the Peter, Paul, Apollos syndrome, a term that I use to describe preacher religion, divisions, factions, and denominational differences in the church body. First, let me lay the blame for the disenchantment with church denominations and with the recent increase in opposition to "organized religion" squarely on Satan, but what is the primary method for such division? The Bible tells us, "Smite the shepherd and the sheep will scatter" (Zechariah 13:7, Matthew 26:31). Note the term *scatter.* The Hebrew word *pasas* or the Greek word *diaskorpizo* both mean "divided, scattered abroad, shaken to pieces, dispersed." The first church wrestled with unity, but all divisions are the result of carnality. Satan takes direct aim at church leadership as the means for the scattering, and the result has been the many denominations and organizations that have developed over the centuries following the founding of the church. Most denominations have a genesis of some charismatic leader that can be traced as the progenitor for the denomination. This is not to claim that such leaders were false prophets or even wrong in their doctrines, but it does claim that there was a differentiation around which adherents coalesced, and many times this could be false doctrines or false personalities.

The Bible declares there is only one Lord, one faith, and one baptism as the true structural identity for the church. Sadly while there are natural differences because of culture or location, there should be no differences in terms of the following:

> With all lowliness and meekness, with long suffering, forbearing one another in love; Endeavoring to keep the unity of the Spirit in the bond of peace. *There is* one body, and one Spirit, even as ye are called in one hope of your calling; One Lord, one faith, one baptism, One God and Father of all, who *is* above all, and through all, and in you all. But unto every one of us is given grace according to the measure of the gift of Christ. Wherefore he saith, when he ascended up on high, he led captivity captive, and gave gifts unto men. (Now that he ascended, what is it but that he also descended first into the lower parts of the earth? He that descended is the same also that ascended up far above all heavens, that he might fill all things.) And he gave some, apostles; and some, prophets; and some, evangelists; and some, pastors and teachers; For the perfecting of the saints, for the work of the ministry, for the

> edifying of the body of Christ: Till we all come
> in the unity of the faith, and of the knowledge
> of the Son of God, unto a perfect man, unto the
> measure of the stature of the fullness of Christ.
> (Ephesians 4:2–13, KJV)

Unfortunately the lack of unity has resulted in man's own way of solving the problem. The "nondenominational" mantra is another cloak of deception in which preacher religion thrives based on personalities and falsehood. Since the key to unity is "one body, one spirit, one Lord, one faith, and one baptism," the concept of "you believe your way and I'll believe mine, and we will both get to heaven at the very same time" is equally wrong. "Nondenominationalism" is a form of ecumenism with false premises of "We all worship the same God" or "Let's love one another and have no doctrine." If the doctrine in the pulpit and the experience in the pew are in any way inconsistent with the spirit and truth of scripture, the fact that there is no denominational attachment matters not.

Multiple denominations or multiple ministerial organizations can be viewed in several ways. It can represent man's efforts to unify with others by establishing a common identity for the church doctrine, culture, or leadership. It can also represent divisions based on church doctrine, culture, or leadership. How it happens, however, is primarily the results of some form of leadership—and often where leadership is at odds with another leadership. Scattered sheep are so often a result of disunity within the ranks of leaders.

The Peter, Paul, Apollos syndrome represents "preacher religion" attributed to division and carnality within the church. How much of the disunity could be attributed to the leadership of Peter, Paul, or Apollos is only conjecture. Certainly there is none that can be attributed to Christ, and based on Paul's writings, it would seem that none of these leaders would be guilty of self-promotion. This begs the question similar to the "chicken or egg first" controversy. Does preacher religion develop because of the behaviors of the preacher or the behaviors and perceptions of the flock?

CHAPTER 15

Avoiding the Pastoral Supremacy Syndrome

Leadership can only exist where there are leaders and followers. Managers do not need followers to fulfill the role of manager unless, of course, it is people they are managing. However, leaders only exist if there are followers. As it has been said, the real definition of leadership is influence, and the major outcomes of leadership exist as both a vision and a relationship. Among the greatest workings of leadership is when a vision becomes a reality, where leaders and followers are unified in a common purpose. I mentioned earlier that the purpose of the church is the reason for its existence, and if the purpose is lost, then the existence of the church does not matter.

The purpose of the church (its mission) is accomplished when ministry (both men and women) carry the message (the vision or gospel) of its leader (Jesus Christ)—and do so by using methods that have been approved or are sanctioned by the highest authority of the church. The primary methods—that is, witnessing, evangelizing, preaching, teaching, and discipleship—are inclusive but not all-inclusive. The spirit of God has shown his approval for many "methods" that adapt to culture, which are not specifically stated in scripture but are different ways that witnessing, preaching, or ministry take place. Tract ministry is not mentioned in scripture but is known to work. Television and radio are methods that have accomplished

God's purpose. God has blessed nursing home ministry, prison ministry, youth ministry—all of which are really preaching the gospel. All of these can work if they stay aligned with God's purpose. However, all of these activities center around the primary method of "gathering in" or "harvesting" those that are called by God into communities that individually are known as "the local church," but is collectively known as "the church," family of God, or body of Christ.

Since the real definition of *church, ekklesia,* as mentioned earlier, is "called to an assembly," relationship is a primary characteristic. The Lord said, "Where two or three are gathered together in my name, there am I in the midst of them" (Matthew 18:20, KJV), which indicates that salvation was never intended to be a solo experience. Neither is Christianity a "go it alone" way of life. The expression "the Lord added to the church daily such as should be saved" (Acts 2:47) only suggests that sowing, reaping, gathering, and assembling are the workings of the church wherever it can be planted. Church planting is a biblical concept that comes from the original leadership vision or mission statement for the gospel of Jesus Christ.

In my earlier discussion on "The Called, Chosen, and Faithful Leader," I posit the first-in-line leader is a visionary and the purpose of leadership is to bring the vision to reality, part of which includes passing the vision to others. This "call to leadership"—that is, the vision itself—must be transferred to followers who will themselves become leaders to carry the vision forward. What was Jesus's vision that would become the vision for the church? In other words, what is the mission statement as it is called in the parlance of organizations? From Isaiah, we read,

> The Spirit of the Lord GOD *is* upon me; because the LORD hath anointed me to preach good tidings unto the meek; he hath sent me to bind up the brokenhearted, to proclaim liberty to the captives, and the opening of the prison to *them that are* bound; To proclaim the acceptable year of the LORD, and the day of vengeance of our God; to comfort all that mourn; To appoint unto

them that mourn in Zion, to give unto them beauty for ashes, the oil of joy for mourning, the garment of praise for the spirit of heaviness; that they might be called trees of righteousness, the planting of the LORD, that he might be glorified. (Isaiah 61:1–3, KJV)

This is the purpose of the church. When Jesus died on Calvary, he purchased the rights of ownership with all equities and assets from the kingdom of heaven to place his gospel in every corner of the world. The spiritual anointing served as the covenant agreement and the written word as the intellectual property that was signed, sealed, and delivered to Jesus Christ and his church. The Lord then appointed the apostles and the disciples that followed, even to us this day, to go into the whole world and plant trees of righteousness, which is one more metaphor for the church, God's people.

The History of Church Planting

Obviously every local church has a beginning. The church in the wilderness began when Moses led Israel out of Egypt. Before that time, Israel was a slave nation, and although they were descendants of Abraham, the covenant promise was not yet fulfilled. The two sons of Abraham, Ishmael and Isaac, were allegorically representing the two national covenants, not the individual covenants, such as it was with Noah or Abraham. The covenant for the nation of Israel began at Sinai, and the covenant for the church began in Jerusalem on Pentecost (Galatians 4:21–31, KJV). However, the blood that was shed that was required for the covenants (or Old and New Testaments) to exist, in both cases, began fifty days earlier—the one for Sinai on Passover night and the one for Jerusalem on the day of crucifixion.

After the church was established in Jerusalem, the disciples, and eventually most of the apostles, were scattered by persecution to other parts of the world. The Acts of the Apostles is the history book of early church plantings. The miracle of the original church of more than 5,000, and later 8,000 more, was not brought about by the preaching of Peter alone. It is interesting to note that for ten days prior to Pentecost, 120 disciples were already assembled; and although most of the time was spent in prayer, we know that some "church business" took place with the selection of Matthias as the replacement for Judas. Whether any preaching or worship went on, the Bible does not say, but it was likely in the context of exhortation, praise, and prayer. The existence of the church must be counted from the day the covenant was opened and read, just as a will or testament is in effect only after the death of the testator and it is unsealed and read before the heirs of the covenant.

Church planting today is in some ways different from the first century in that while the purpose of planting is to spread the gospel message through evangelizing, many churches come into existence by means of membership transfer rather than conversion of sinners. In a class on evangelism at Liberty University, Dr. Wheeler (2010) shared research statistics that should be of notable concern to Christians. First, North America is the only world continent where Christianity is not growing. The U.S. population increased 11.4 percent in the ten years prior to the study, while church membership declined by 9.5 percent. According to the study, evangelical churches failed to gain 2 percent of the population of the United States in the past fifty years. The most astounding note, however, is that during the previous ten-year period, over half of the churches in the United States did not gain one new church member by conversion. Most churches only grew by transfer. Furthermore, a study done in 1990 by the Southern Baptist, the largest evangelical church in America, found that 60 percent of baptisms in churches were rebaptisms rather than new baptisms.[94]

The reality is that most new churches that open their doors do not happen as a result of true evangelism and conversion. Many are communities of disenfranchised believers that break away from

---

[94.] Dr. David Wheeler, "Introduction to Servant Evangelism," a Course from Liberty University, January 2010.

already existing churches. Others are churches that open and grow by personality shoppers. Some church start-ups are remnant believers of churches that have closed, and new pastors have been sent by God to care for the scattered flock that had once existed. While this is not the case as much in foreign missions, most churches in the United States are the gatherings of existing Christians. One caveat however—many Christians are in name only and need conversion. However, there are great blessings for those church planting where true conversions do result from the new ministry. The heart of a true evangelistic ministry is one, like Paul, who says,

> For I will not dare to speak of any of those things which Christ hath not wrought by me, to make the Gentiles obedient, by word and deed, Through mighty signs and wonders, by the power of the Spirit of God; so that from Jerusalem, and round about unto Illyricum, I have fully preached the gospel of Christ. Yea, so have I strived to preach the gospel, not where Christ was named, lest I should build upon another man's foundation: But as it is written, To whom he was not spoken of, they shall see: and they that have not heard shall understand. (Romans 15:18–21, KJV)

One difference of concern between the planting of churches in the first century and those of today is the sad—and what I believe is unethical—practice of churches of the same faith being planted down the street from a sister church to draw away members. This unethical practice is fostered by the single-pastor concept, where ministries compete for the flock. "Sheep stealing," as it has been called, does happen; and while some justify the behavior, it calls to our attention the problems of the Peter, Paul, Apollos syndrome, where divisiveness exists and where pastors or preachers fail to understand the benefits of collegial eldership. The unwillingness of ministers of the gospel to work with other ministers of the gospel has resulted in the proliferation of the kingdom of God, but does it really indicate division? Again, Paul noted,

> Some indeed preach Christ even of envy and strife; and some also of good will: The one preach Christ of contention, not sincerely, supposing to affliction to my bonds: But the other of love, knowing that I am set for the defense of the gospel. What then? Notwithstanding, every way, whether in pretense, or in truth, Christ is preached; and I therein do rejoice, yea, and will rejoice. (Philippians 1:15–18)

While there are many motives behind church planting, the work begun by divisiveness will be as the wood, hay, and stubble that will be tried by fire (1 Corinthians 3:11–15).

Biblical Church Planting

The book of Acts is the account of church planting, primarily by Peter, Paul, and their associate ministers. Some accounts, such as the story of Peter preaching to Cornelius's family, or even the story of Philip's preaching in Samaria, do not detail much more than the conversions as a result of evangelism. The church growth from those times of evangelism must only be assumed. We do not know who the church leaders were, whether there was a single pastor or collegial leadership that took shape in the church. We do not know where they met—a house or another building. We know the structure of the Jerusalem church, with its collegial eldership and meeting house to house and in the temple. We know its chief leadership structure only by Paul's reference to Peter, James, and John as pillars, along with apostles and other elders. How many elders are not known? We know apostles and deacons went out from the church to preach the gospel in keeping with the Lord's instruction, "in Jerusalem, and in all Judea, and in Samaria, and unto the uttermost parts of the earth" (Acts 1:8, KJV).

After Philip's revival in Samaria, we read that Philip "preached in all the cities" until he settled in Caesarea (Acts 8:40). Jesus prepared the way for Philip's revival the story of the woman at the well (John 4), so it is likely there were believers in Jesus, the Messiah, that were part of Philip's revival. According to Catholic tradition, Prochorus, one of the first church deacons listed among the seven in Acts 6, and who was the nephew of Stephen, played a significant role in the development of the church in Samaria. Philip's residence in Caesarea, however, coincided with the conversion of Cornelius, also in Caesarea, and it is likely that Philip, along with Cornelius and his family, were leaders in the Church of Caesarea. The *Apostolic Constitutions*, eight treatises of church history, state that early "bishops" of Caesarea included Zacchaeus the publican, Cornelius, and Theophilus (the recipient of Luke's letters).

Early church growth prior to the missionary journeys of Paul included saints in Damascus, Lydda, Saron, and Joppa (Acts 9). The conversion of Cornelius in Caesarea is recorded in chapters 10 and 11 of Acts. Christianity spread to Phenice, Cyprus, and Antioch. It is in Antioch that we first read of collegial elders, other than those in Jerusalem (Acts 13:1, KJV). However, we also note that it was in Antioch that Paul and Barnabas were sent out as a team to be apostles to the Gentiles. The Bible also speaks of John Mark being a part of the ministry team.

The book of Acts covers three missionary journeys of Paul, tells how elders were appointed in local churches, and records that Paul and Barnabas, apostles who were the planters of churches, ministered in cohort with others. There is the suggestion of team ministry in the Lord's earliest evangelism. In the book of Acts, a pattern of team ministry was the norm, not the exception. Could there be significance or purpose for the Lord's choice of sending his disciples two by two (Mark 6:7, Luke 10:1), in his early ministry? The apostles appear to continue this practice of teams in the missionary journeys recorded in the book of Acts. Why did the Lord say, "Separate me Barnabas and Saul for the work where unto I have called them" (Acts

13:2, KJV). Why did he not send Saul (Paul) alone? We will not conclude that the Lord feared miscreant conduct, attitudes, or pride in the lives of either of these men, but more likely the answer is that the work of missionaries (church planters) is always greater than a person could or should do alone. The danger or damage to the spiritual man with such a heavy load is more than average, and unless those in ministry know how to adapt to God's framework of ministry, eventually trouble will ensue that creates a maladaptive approach to God's plan for leadership.

The first commonplace problem in church planting is founder's syndrome, which leads to the second commonplace problem in churches today, the pastoral supremacy syndrome—both of which relate to centralized power structures. Unless spiritual leadership has the humility of Moses, the results can be one of spiritual abuse and will ultimately contribute to the demise of the fivefold ministerial gifts or other spiritual gifts within the congregation. Talents may continue to exist and reign, but God's spiritual blessings will be overshadowed and diminished as Jesus and his angelic host are being replaced by human efforts that attract and mislead believers.

Founder's Syndrome

Block and Rosenberg (2002) write, "Founder's syndrome refers to the influential powers and privileges that the founder exercises or that others attribute to the founder."[95] The authors also note, "Founders deserve special recognition because they have demonstrated a remarkable capacity to translate their visionary ideas into organizational realities for the good of the community."[96] What is the first error in logic that can be noted in the discussion when it comes to founders of churches? First is that church planters are not

---

[95] Stephen R. Block and Steven A. Rosenberg, "Toward an Understanding of Founder's Syndrome: An Assessment of Power and Privilege among Founders of Non-Profit Organizations," *Non-Profit Management and Leadership* 12, no. 4 (2002): 353–368.

[96] Block and Rosenberg, 353.

really the founders of the church. The vision is not really their vision, yet in the norm, the most likely scenario is that the church planter does have a vision and acts upon that vision. The question is whether the vision is one that is received from God and aligns with God's purposes for that particular planting, or is the founder of the church acting upon his or her own vision?

Eddleman (2011) writes, "In his book *Leadership and Supervision in Business*, Carter McNamara, MBA, PhD, describes FS [founder's syndrome] as a condition in which an organization operates primarily according to the personalities of one or more members, usually the founders, rather than according to the organization's mission, policies, and systems."[97] Eddleman notes that control systems, lines of authority, budgets, and strategic planning are important elements of an organization, but progress in reaching the organizations potential is impeded when founders fear losing control of these processes.

I mentioned in the beginning of this book that the biggest problem in the ministry today is the minister's self-involvement with the message and all else that can be attributed to the calling of God. When God calls a man or a woman to ministry, he is sharing his vision with those he calls. The first-in-line leader, the visionary, has within the heart a purpose, a plan, and goals that are intended to bring the vision to reality. The ministry must carry out the vision for God, requiring constant communication with the true head of the church, Jesus Christ. The pastoral supremacy syndrome assumes the role as the head of the church, and in various ways it promotes the "headship" of the pastor rather than the headship of Christ.

Founder's syndrome actually represents leadership failure in the most important function of leadership—mentoring followers to become leaders. One difference between leadership and management is the character of authority as it is used in a relationship. Management often entails positional authority that is a structured task, while leadership authority is based on the condition of the

---

[97.] D. Kirk Eddleman, "Founder's Syndrome: Most Frequently Seen in Entrepreneurial Practices, This Condition Can Cripple Your Performance," *EquiManagement Summer*, May issue (2011): 12–13.

relationship. Management authority tends to be static, full of expectations that are defined by rules and roles. Leadership authority is dynamic, and while positions and roles are a factor, it is a matter of influence and is determined by how relationship factors exist. Strong relationships have great advantage in leadership, while weak relationships must use intermediate relationships to make leadership work more effectively. The danger of founder's syndrome is that insecure leaders rely on political maneuvering to maintain their leadership role. Authority, even that which is delegated, is restricted, which leads to role confusion—and eventually turns into a leadership crisis. Under founder's syndrome, often the best of leaders eventually will leave a church, while many of those that otherwise remain become passive, subservient yes-men, who will tend to contribute less to the benefit of the organization.

There are several characteristics of founder's syndrome that develop within organizations, and these will cripple the growth of the church and also impede the development of the fivefold ministry. When considering that the fivefold ministry often leads the church into fulfilling the ministry of the whole church, the ability of others to mentor leaders is also restricted. The church will eventually depend on "talent," not "gifts," in trying to do the work of God. Here is a list of the syndrome's characteristics:

- Founders resist delegating authority or tend to highly control the authority that is delegated, which leads to role confusion on the part of other leaders, mentors, or followers.
- Succession planning is often lacking, or family dynasties occur, which results in overidentification with the founder and not with Jesus Christ.
- Founders will often get in the way of growth and maturity in the organization, fearing loss of control.
- Personal agendas replace organizational vision and mission.
- Leadership crises are a recurring theme as there is a lack of balance in leadership and accountability for organizational leadership. This can lead to ethical crises within the church.

- Leadership becomes political in nature, based on nepotism or favoritism rather than on allowing God to promote spiritual gifts. Supporters of leadership are based on loyalty to the leader, not on the gifts or abilities that promote organizational growth and maturity.
- Founders use symbolism to self-promote or enhance personal identity with the organization. Churches refer to the church by the pastor's name; references to the church by other identify any association by the founder. There is a lifting up of the ministry rather than a lifting up of Christ.
- Decision making is often based on crisis management or reactive rather than strategic.

While there are many leaders who are adept at avoiding the pitfalls of founder's syndrome and their character or temperament works well with others with leadership skills, the demise of the five-fold ministry, the false narrative of a single-pastor church, the promulgation of pastoral appreciation days, and the rise of talents that replace spiritual gifts operating within the church are all marks that founder's syndrome has been rooted deep within the organizational structure of Christian churches and hinders the real work of God. The monumental rise of television evangelists, "worshiptainment," preacher religion, and the blind leading the blind are but many examples of this epidemic.

Pastoral Supremacy Syndrome

Pastoral supremacy syndrome is a later stage of founder's syndrome, but even more, it is an ideology that has become entrenched in the rank and file of both the leadership and the members of churches. Following my own experience of going through a church breakup, I continued to plant churches and pastor them, but in doing so, I attempted to implement collegial eldership in my latter efforts. I found resistance, not only by ministers that I tried to mentor, but also by members of the church who were not familiar with the concept. While there are some churches who have used elders and a more Presbyterian polity of church leadership, many evangelical churches are most familiar with a single-pastor-led church. Many pastors have taught on the fivefold ministry but have never experienced the realities of fivefold ministry.

In the earlier years of Pentecost, there were men and women who were deemed as prophets, and a few as apostles, but the general designation for decades has been that the prominent church role is that of a pastor as a single leader. Where elders were a part of the church, those serving as "elder boards" would be seen in different ways, either as sitting above or below the pastoral ministry, depending on the governing structure. At times, tensions would exist as ministers felt that elder boards expected pastors to be the "hirelings" instead of true shepherds. Most often boards in single-led churches were "loyalty positions." Some of the symptoms of the pastoral supremacy syndrome include the following:

- All the characteristics entailed in the aforementioned founder's syndrome
- Dynasty or kingdom building
- Levels of hierarchy within ministerial bodies
- The creation of status symbols, privileges, and benefits that exist only for the pastor but not for other ministers in the church, such as pastoral appreciation days, new cars, and, yes, housing allowances
- Centralized authority and decision making with little input from advisers
- Strong control of church finances and financial processes

It is true that there are indeed benefits both from the biblical perspective and from the regulatory environment for ministers of the gospel. The biblical structure of fivefold ministry and also of church governance supports the concept of the "laborer is worthy of his hire," and for that reason, the Bible does declare that those that labor in the Word and doctrine should receive double honor, referring to remuneration. However, both structures are intended by

God to be in the plural, which in essence would minimize excessive abuses. Of course, that does leave open the question, "How many parsonages should be built?" How did Israel handle such a question for the Levites and priesthood?

Missions the Hard Way

Whatever happened to the apostolic teams that started churches in the New Testament? What about Jesus sending out his disciples two at a time, even when he sent the seventy? How many apostles and elders were in the Jerusalem church? One argument that always arises is, "Jerusalem had multiple preaching sites, and each preaching site had a pastor." The same was in Ephesus, where Timothy was the pastor.

Many want to use the argument that the plurality of elders always meant that an "elder" was just another term for a pastor and that it referred to elders working in separate locations in a city. Supposing that argument was true, then I can only say it would be an evidence of us not working scripturally because most pastors in most cities do not share oversight for the church corporate. We are blind indeed if we think that churches work together in most cities.

But consider that argument in light of the scripture that says, "Is any sick among you, let him call for the elders of the church, and let them pray over him, anointing him with oil in the name of the Lord" (James 5:14). Using the argument just given, we are to gather all the pastors from each of the local apostolic churches to come pray for our sick.

No, you say it is all right to have elders in the local church. But since there are very few apostolic churches that have real elders, we encourage any of the saints to come lay hands on the sick as a substitute. How wonderful it would be, I think, if two or more families worked together to start a church rather than just one. But it would also be wonderful if men who had the call of home missions would develop men who would become elders and had John the Baptist's understanding—"He must increase, but I must decrease."

I believe that Jesus Christ will only increase as men decrease. I don't see how this is possible in churches where the single-pastor concept is fostered to the exclusion or subordination of other ministries. Biblically there is not one scripture that supports the elevation of the pastoral ministry above the other ministries. Many will denounce the concept of collegial eldership, but this is the crisis. We are far removed from scriptural principles in church government and in the recognition and operation of all the ministerial gifts.

CHAPTER 16

The Awakening

Following my salvation experience, Jesus Christ called me to preach during a prayer vigil in the United Pentecostal Church in Baytown, Texas. I was baptized in Jesus's name and received the Holy Spirit in a revival preached by Wayne Huntley for Brother Lonnie Marcus. The Lord led my steps in many peculiar ways, but I was very blessed to be under the teaching and preaching of some of the finest men in the apostolic movement—men like Corliss Dees, Lonnie Treadway, Lonnie Marcus, and Leo Paul Upton. All of these men were tremendous ministers and had one thing in common—all were leaders among men, great administrators as well as great ministers.

During the next twenty years, I became a home missionary, opening new works in New York, Rhode Island, Virginia, and Pennsylvania. I soon discovered that I had many weaknesses, but I also found that the Lord could do great work even with all of my weaknesses and failures. I discovered as well that I had this constant desire to do things my own way instead of doing it God's way. I was able to lead. I was able to build. I was able to organize and direct—supervise, administer. Many of the things that I had seen other—some more successful—ministers and pastors do so effectively. The hardest thing for me to do was serve.

This became the most evident in Rhode Island, where my family and I experienced some of the most wonderful miracles in starting a new church. It was in Louisiana that the Lord directed me to move to the city of Woonsocket, Rhode Island. I had never heard of the place, but by faith, I loaded my wife and two young children and moved to the city of Woonsocket in a small trailer towed behind my car. We had no furniture, no job, and no contacts in the city. Little did I realize that in the city of Woonsocket was a young group of baptized born-again, one-God believers meeting in the basement of a home, praying for a pastor. At the same time, there was a young couple originally from that town that had been living in Memphis, Tennessee, but now returning to the city of Woonsocket. They, too, were praying that there would be a church there.

I found an apartment for $30 a week on the third floor of a housing unit where several other families lived. Woonsocket was a crowded city of fifty thousand, rich in French Canadian heritage. It was also notably Catholic from one border of town to the next. Although there were a few non-Catholic churches in town, Woonsocket has some of the most beautiful Catholic edifices in the state, with thriving congregations and a large number of Catholic charismatics as well.

Within the first month, while I visited a sister church in Worcester, Massachusetts, I met one of the young men whose family was praying for a church to be established in Woonsocket. There was no pastor at the time, but three of the men had been ordained as elders by an elderly apostolic preacher who had at one time been with the group. It was also in that first month that I witnessed to a young Catholic man whose father was a "lay minister" in the Catholic charismatic movement. I was immediately invited to preach for that group, and we baptized eleven individuals from that first service. By the end of the second month, we had nearly fifty in Sunday school and were renting a Knights of Columbus hall for church services.

I won't take all the time to tell of the church growth, the miracles that provided a new building, nor of many other miracles. But we also had our trials. It was during this time that I was introduced to the concept of the plurality of elders by two "co-pastors" of the church in Worcester. In spite of all that I had been taught, I could not deny that the scriptures teach consistently that it was a plurality of elders that were to be the overseers of the New Testament church.

- Acts 14:23 (KJV)—And when they had ordained them elders in every church, and had prayed with fasting, they commended them to the Lord, on whom they believed.
- Acts 20:17 (KJV)—And from Miletus he sent to Ephesus and called the elders of the church.
- Acts 20:27–28 (KJV)—For I have not shunned to declare unto you all the counsel of God. Take heed therefore unto yourselves, and to all the flock, over the which the Holy Ghost hath made you overseers, to feed the church of God, which he hath purchased with his own blood.
- 1 Timothy 5:17 (KJV)—Let the elders that rule well be counted worthy of double honour, especially they who labour in the word and doctrine.
- Titus 1:5 (KJV)—For this cause left I thee in Crete, that thou shouldest set in order the things that are wanting, and ordain elders in every city, as I had appointed thee.
- James 5:14 (KJV)—Is any sick among you? let him call for the elders of the church; and let them pray over him, anointing him with oil in the name of the Lord.
- Hebrews 13:17 (KJV)—Obey them that have the rule over you, and submit yourselves: for they watch for your souls, as they that must give account, that they may do it with joy, and not with grief: for that is unprofitable for you.

However, I worked with the three "elders" of our church in the old-fashioned way as "senior pastor," or "pastor" over the elders. This was done on the premise that there could only be "one pastor" and "anything with two heads is a monster." Eventually my nonbiblical approach to protecting my "God-given right of leadership" cost me dearly when the church split over differences of opinion.

Let me point out here that God never intended for there to be differences of opinion that would divide the church. What God wants is that differences of opinion would give way to unity of understanding—in which God's right answer is eventually reached through prayer, love, study, and relationship. I could be totally right and a brother totally wrong, and the end result should be that the brother in the wrong will come to the right while unity and the relationship is being maintained. I am not advocating holding a wrong point of view or accepting the wrong point of view. I am advocating a loving relationship while the errant party is discovering the truth (2 Timothy 2:24–26, Ephesians 4:13).

I did not do that. I was the pastor, and as such, I was to be right in what I had to say. I was advised to not allow the "elders" the upper hand or they would "overthrow" the pastor. How wrong is this approach or this thinking? The oversight of the church is not in the hands of one man other than Jesus Christ alone. Jesus is the only "One" or "I Am"—where the buck stops. The buck does not stop with the pastor. Whoever feels that this is the case is stopping one level short. There is only One Shepherd that is above all the church, and all the elders, pastors, apostles, evangelists, teachers, and prophets are undershepherds who oversee the church on an equal basis.

The Church in Crisis

With the pain and failure of a church split, not only did I find myself leaving Rhode Island, but I had opportunities then and later to consider what I considered one of my greatest failures. I readily admit that I was spiritually low, leaning toward carnality, making mistakes and errors in judgment. But worse was the fact that my pride was preventing me from doing the right thing, which would have kept the church together and—I believe—would have brought a greater revival to Rhode Island. I did not submit to the brothers who were not only ordained elders in the church but in a much better spiritual condition than I was at that time.

Let me point out a repeated problem for many preachers. Because we have it in our head that we must be the head of the local church, when we are "pastors," it is easier and more face-saving to move on than to sit down and submit to other men who were called to work with us in the church where we are leaders. The problem is that we carry our baggage and mistakes with us, and we will often repeat the same error simply because of our erroneous understanding of being "the pastor." Note that I did not say "a pastor."

Over the next several years, I did a thorough study of the scriptures concerning pastoring, plurality of elders, and the apostolic ministry. I continued to start churches as one man (still not given over entirely to a new concept), but wanting more and more that starting churches could be easier. Also I began to see more clearly why the single-pastor concept was totally contrary to scripture.

No One Can Tell Me What to Do but the Pastor

Like the apostle Paul, I needed a home church when I was not "pastoring." Texas is my home state, and after several years in the Northeast, my family and I returned to Texas to live there for a while. We attended a small church in East Texas. When we first arrived, the pastor of the church treated my family with dignity and was such a blessing for us. Eventually he left to become the pastor of a larger church in Houston. He certainly had "what it takes" to do the job.

The second pastor during our stay was another wonderful man—a good preacher, a caring and loving man, and a gentleman. I can say that both of these pastors were doing a fine job. Unfortunately, there was little growth, little revival, and little actual working of spiritual gifts except what is normally seen in our churches today. Preaching is a gift, and we do see that. A person receiving the Holy Ghost still continues to be a miracle. But there is little "prophecy," an occasional healing, and miracles even less. Instead we have "normal church."

While in the church in East Texas, my family became close to another one of the families, and as we often did, we were having dinner at their house. On one occasion, the dear sister for whatever reason rebuked her husband in a manner that would be considered entirely inappropriate according to scripture. I then admonished this sister concerning this behavior because it was an ungodly behavior according to the scripture. Her response to me was, "You can't tell me what to do. No one can tell me but the pastor."

Later I had a chance to recount the incident to the pastor of the church. At that moment, I asked him this question, "Brother, when the apostle Paul was between missionary journeys, he would return to his home church in Antioch. Was he not an apostle while he sat on the pew or while he was at home? Why is that we think that when a man is between pastoring churches, he is not a pastor?"

The answer is simple. Our definition of a pastor is relative to an office, rather than being considered a ministerial gift. It is okay to have more than one apostle in a local church (providing of course that we believe in apostles for today). You cannot say otherwise and agree with the scriptures. It is clearly evident that the church in Jerusalem had more than one apostle working together in that church. It is also clearly evident that there were multiple prophets and teachers in the Antioch church (Acts 13:1). So why is it that a local church can have more than one apostle, more than one prophet, more than one teacher, more than one evangelist—but only one pastor? At the same time, it is clearly inconceivable that when there are multiples of these ministries in any local church, only one of them can operate in that gift there, while the others must refrain from exercising their gifts.

But I Am a Pastor, You Know

I heard of this incident, and since it is hearsay, I can only paraphrase my understanding of what may have been said. At a ministerial conference, I understand that one of our best apostolic preachers was being introduced as the guest speaker. This brother for years had been an evangelist but at this time had been a seasoned pastor for many years. I understand that he was introduced as "evangelist so and so."

When the brother came to the pulpit, it is reported that he said, "But I am a pastor, you know." The message was clear that he felt this had to be clarified for him to have validity to preach to all these preachers.

Early in my ministry, I was on the evangelistic field full-time. During that time and ever since, I have had opportunities to attend many sectional, district, and general conferences. For the most part, pastors are elevated and set apart above all other ministries. I can remember getting a certain amount of recognition because I was a special speaker or good evangelist, but there was always an understanding the evangelist did not have equality with pastors.

Take note that in most conferences today, the pastors still have a somewhat separate recognition. Seldom if ever are apostles recognized, or prophets, or teachers. Seldom do "assistant pastors" get recognized equally as a coworker in the ministry. The fact of the matter is that pastors have been elevated to the first of the fivefold (or fourfold) ministries, while the single-pastor concept has practically wiped out the functionality of the other ministries listed in Ephesians 4:11.

This is the crisis—the church is making extinct the understanding of spiritual ministerial gifts. The term *pastor* now refers to an office, not a function. And I feel that most pastors do not have a clear understanding of the distinction between apostle and pastor, or prophet and pastor.

It is interesting to note that in the scriptures, we can see evidence of apostles, evangelists, and prophets as they minister in their callings. There is not one person called a pastor in the New Testament other than Jesus Christ. The title of pastor is not specifically identified with any individual in the New Testament church, while there are clear and specific accounts of men who function in the other ministries. Yet pastor has been elevated above all the rest. What we see is a clear example of a spirit that manifested itself in Diotrephes when he wanted preeminence in the local church (3 John 1:9).

Who Gets the Tithes?

Some of the problems with having more than one pastor is how do you divide the tithes? How do you divide the pulpit? How do you divide the power? Some preachers teach that the pastor gets all of the tithes. What if you have an apostle in the church? What of the teachers? Scripturally we have evidence that "they that preach the gospel should live of the gospel," and this was written for the sake of the apostle Paul (1 Corinthians 9:14, KJV). We can also find that the support of ministries applied to a plurality of elders (1 Timothy 5:17–18). A modern version of support is "pastors get tithes, missionaries (apostles) and evangelists get offerings, prophets and teachers get nothing."

I have experienced more than once that it was expected that visiting ministers would receive an offering from the local church. But I also have experienced that it was expected that if you were a minister in the local church and had an opportunity to preach or teach Sunday school, this was to be done without remuneration—this was a privilege but not worthy of reward. Often the pastor would be the only minister in the local church receiving remuneration.

I remember one church that I pastored for a short time that had a fair-sized congregation of over one hundred saints, but the church board consisted of one family of a mother, a father, and seven sons. The father and sons made up the church board, but the power was in the hands of the mother. The church had a fine man as a pastor, but when a disagreement between the mother and the pastor arose, he was fired from the position. When the vacancy arose, and because I was preaching in the state, I was asked to fill in to minister to the church. Prophecy went forth in the service (it was only my first time there), and the service went in such a manner that I was asked to be considered for the pastoral position. I was voted in as the pastor, and one of the first surprises for the church was when I refused to receive all the tithes. The tithing was substantial, and the church had been trained that the pastor got all of the tithing and the offering supported the work of the church. I insisted the tithing go into the general fund and I would receive a modest salary far below the amount of tithing. This allowed the church to provide for other ministries in evangelist that preached for the church.

Sadly many interpret Paul's instructions to Timothy—"Let the elders that preach once in a while…"—by conveniently leaving out the rest of the scripture. It does not say, "Let the elders that preach once in a while be counted worthy of double honor." It clearly says, "Let the elders that rule well be counted worthy of double honor."

The job description for an elder is to rule, to oversee, and to supervise, and this is always given in the plural case, never singularly.

Obviously churches must consider the budgets and financial realities of a local church. Many founding pastors work hard in secular vocations until the church is financially capable of supporting a full-time minister. It stands to reason that the elder who has been overseeing the church (whether pastor, evangelist, or another of the fivefold ministry) should be the first in line to receive from the tithes and offerings of the church. However, if there is collegial eldership, as the Bible teaches, then the church is to distribute the tithes evenly, with preaching elders having a double portion. One suggestion is that the ministry should not receive in salary above and beyond the average wages of those that are members of the church. The excesses often seen in ministry reflect poorly on the ministry and suggest the "appearance of evil." What must change in churches today is the practice of using ministers that are members of the church to preach in the pulpits with disregard for the Lord's injunction, "The laborer is worthy of his hire" (Luke 10:7). The typical practice of only taking up offerings for visiting preachers while not providing the same for ministers in the church other than the pastor falls short of biblical practice.

One caveat here—pastors must avoid thinking to themselves, "I will just not use another preacher in the church and that way I can avoid paying them." It is common for ministers to move from out of the area and find themselves in a local church. Should a minister who has been proven in ministry become a part of another church, unless there is a reason not to use them, they should receive the honor due them. There is a scripture about tithing that deals with just this subject, where one minister comes from another place and becomes a part of another community:

> And if a Levite come from any of thy gates out of all Israel, where he sojourned, and come with all the desire of his mind unto the place which the LORD shall choose; Then he shall minister in the name of the LORD his God, as all his

brethren the Levites do, which stand there before
the LORD. They shall have like portions to eat,
beside that which cometh of the sale of his patri-
mony. (Deuteronomy 18:6–8, KJV)

Obviously this can be a sensitive subject. First, we know that
just because a person claims to be a preacher does not make them
one. The Bible gives admonition to "know those who labor among
you," but if indeed a person's ministry is known and established to be
such, if they labor in the ministry in a local church where they have
settled, the laborer is still worthy of his hire. The verse in 1 Timothy
5:17 covers the case of one who becomes an "elder" in the church.

CHAPTER 17

The Fivefold Ministry

There has been disagreement among many today concerning the nature and number of ministries that exist in the New Testament church. Most Evangelical, Pentecostal, and Apostolic churches accept the term *pastor* for their primary minister. The evangelist is usually defined as a traveling minister, and teacher can apply to just about anybody who teaches in the local church—unless they become famous and then the title might be added to their resume or ad lines when doing seminars or special services.

On the other hand, Ephesians 4:11 speaks of several different ministries given to the church as "gifts." We read, "And he gave some, apostles; and some, prophets; and some, evangelists; and some, pastors and teachers—". Some groups see this scripture as referring to a "Fivefold Ministry," while still others see the last two (pastors and teachers) as being one ministry, thus recognizing a "Four-Fold Ministry." In reality, few churches today are willing to call anyone an "Apostle" with a few exceptions.

Some Christian churches teach that the Apostle and Prophet are early New Testament ministries that were to cease at the end of a time period called the Apostolic Age. The Bible does not speak of an *apostolic age*, nor does it teach that the Lord intended for his church to change message or ministry while the church existed in this world. This same teaching is parallel to the idea that prophecy, tongues, and interpretations have all ceased at some point near the beginning of the church age—probably after the death of the last living original apostle, John, who wrote the book of Revelation.

The Bible however declares that both message and ministry would continue for as long as the church is in this present world. When speaking of the spiritual gifts that were imparted to the church, Paul declares in 1 Corinthians 1:7, "So that you come behind in no gift waiting for the coming of the Lord Jesus Christ." Jesus Christ himself is "the same, yesterday, today, and forever" (Hebrews 13:8). The basic reason for teaching the cessation of gifts is rooted in the idea that knowledge gained through the written Word is equal and even superior to the power of the church before the Bible was printed.

However, I believe that any church that no longer recognizes the exercise of spiritual gifts, whether those given in the form of vocal gifts or those given in the form of power gifts, is far removed from the design that God gave and should not be counted as a part of God's true church. Instead they fulfill the scripture that speak of those that have a "form of godliness but denying the power thereof" and we are admonished to turn away from such a teaching (2 Timothy 3:5).

Whether Ephesians 4:11 is speaking of a "Fivefold" or a "Four-Fold" ministry is not important when we understand that this scripture is not defining offices but speaking of types of ministry. The very reason why there is confusion is that each of these ministries is seen more as a specific office to be held rather than a ministry of service. Many think of the office of the apostle and the office of the pastor as something to elevate rather than truly seeing how these are ministries that serve the body of Jesus Christ.

The Hand Ministry

One writer has described the fivefold ministry (or four-fold, if you like) as "the hand ministry." Using the five fingers of the hand, he describes it this way:

- The Apostle for Governing
- The Prophet for Guiding

- The Evangelist for Gathering
- The Pastor for Guarding
- The Teacher for Grounding

Notice that this associates each ministry with a function, not an office. Each function works together like the fingers of the hand to do the work. It might be noted that of all the parts of the body, the one that does the most work of any kind is that of the hand. It is the body's natural tool or instrument of work. Regardless of what industry we are in from clerical administration to surgeon, the hand is the basic body part on which we depend the most.

CHAPTER 18

The Apostle

First of all, let us set the record straight about apostles. There has not been a cessation of this kind of ministry in the church. Although there were twelve duly appointed by Jesus Christ as a part of the foundation of the church, the number was not limited to twelve and did not cease with twelve. Here are a few other apostles mentioned by name in the New Testament Church:

1. Acts 1:26—Matthias was the replacement for Judas. The qualification for Matthias was that he had to be chosen from among those who were in the company of the rest of the apostles from the time of John the Baptist until the ascension of Jesus Christ (verses 21 and 22). This was not the qualification for all apostles, otherwise Paul could not have been later considered as an Apostle, neither Barnabas who was also an apostle. (Acts 14:14)

2. Acts 14:14—Paul, Saul of Tarsus (later to be called Paul), was not one of the original twelve mentioned in the gospels but was later chosen by God. Many feel that his mention of the fact that he had "seen" Jesus in 1 Corinthians 9:1 was a statement of an explicit qualification for apostle-

ship. This may or may not be the case. Certainly, Paul did not meet the other qualifications mentioned in Acts 1:21 and 22 that Matthias had to meet. I do not believe that Matthias' qualifications were for all apostles but only to be numbered among the original twelve. And I do not believe that "seeing the Lord" as Paul did was also a qualification for all apostles. We do not know whether Apollos, or Barnabas, or Timothy, who were also apostles, ever "saw the Lord," but we also do not know that they didn't. We also need to realize that it is very possible that the Lord could appear to men today. There is no indication in the scripture that he would stop doing so.

3. Acts 14:14 Barnabas is called an apostle. Also see 1 Corinthians 9:6 in the context of apostleship. Barnabas is given the same right hand and perceived commission in Galatians 2:9—he was also considered an apostle to the Gentiles.

4. 1 Corinthians 4:6–9—Paul speaks of Apollos, and says "God hath set forth us the apostles last, as it were appointed to death."

5. Galatians 1:19—James, the Lord's brother (not the James that was the brother of John who was killed by Herod in Acts 12:2). This is the same James who wrote the book of James and who was also considered as one of the pillars of the church.

6. 1 Thessalonians 1:1 compared to 2:6—Silas and Timothy are listed in verse 1 and referred to as the "we the apostles" in 2:6.

7. 2 Corinthians 8:23—Titus is called one of the messengers to the church. The word messenger is from the Greek "*apostolos.*"

8. Philippians 2:25—the same word, messenger or "apostolos," is used for Epaphroditus.

What of the other ministries mentioned in Ephesians 4:11? As already mentioned, we have seen that Agabus was listed as a prophet and Acts 13:1 speaks of several prophets and teachers. The only evangelist mentioned by name is Philip who was originally among the seven chosen in Acts 6 to take care of the daily care of service to the widows. It is often thought that these seven were the first "deacons" in the church. However, both Stephen and Philip out of that group were heavily anointed and preached the gospel. Stephen was soon martyred, but Philip began to preach in Samaria when the church came under persecution and fled Jerusalem (Acts 8).

Philip's message was the simple gospel of Jesus Christ— "preaching the things concerning the kingdom of God and the name of Jesus Christ" (Acts 8:12), which led to the baptism of new converts. First it was in Samaria, and then he was led to preach to the Eunuch from Ethiopia in the desert. Next, he preached in all the cities near Azotus, and finally Philip settles in Caesarea. According to Acts 21:8–9, Philip was known as the "evangelist" who had four daughters that had the gift of prophecy.

What stands out in the New Testament is that whereas there is at least one example of four of the ministries mentioned in Ephesians 4:11, there is not one person in the New Testament who was given the title "Pastor." This may be one reason why some sees the terms "pastors and teachers" as one ministry. One thing is certain; this ministry did exist because the Bible says so in this verse.

What Is an Apostle?

Yes, apostles do exist today. The word "*apostolos*" simply meant messenger, as we have already stated. The foreign missionaries that have been ordained, appointed, and sent out by the United Pentecostal Church, Assemblies of the Lord Jesus, or other apostolic organization are in truth apostles.

Notice that one of the duties of the apostle is to ordain elders in every church (Acts 14:23). Our foreign missionaries go into another country and do more than just evangelize the lost. They focus on developing national ministers. Their calling is to more than just a local city, but to a country or region. In starting Bible Colleges and in overseeing more than one work, all the functions that we see in the apostolic ministry as evidenced in Paul, Apollos, and Barnabas exist in the missionaries of today.

The apostles are responsible for explaining and protecting doctrine, for mentoring preachers—not just saints. There is a greater gift to disciple, I believe in the ministry of the apostles, than in any of the other ministerial gifts. This is not to say that discipleship does not exist. It just seems to be more pronounced and developed in the man who is gifted with the missionary calling—i.e., apostle.

Another function of the apostle was to govern—not on the local level but on a broader level. Paul had powers of correction that he most assuredly referred to while refraining to exercise the authority that he was given. Sometimes we may feel that as ministers, our votes make a General Superintendent or District Superintendent. Perhaps they do, but I also feel that God does bring influence to bear on certain leadership roles that are of a broader nature, and that God has often ordained the vote to go toward a particular individual that is appointed to that office.

That doesn't mean that mistakes don't happen, and even wrong elections are made. But if we can only look at the spiritual impact of many of these men on the body or the organization and understand that there has been some spiritual substance to how they were gifted to provide leadership.

I am not concluding, however, that all men who obtain an organizational leadership role in a district, conference, or national organization are apostles. Many will have the titles, and maybe administrative and organizational ability that gets them where they are. But I do believe that there are some who really have an apostolic gift, and they excel. In time we will know when we receive our rewards.

CHAPTER 19

The Prophet

Who was the greatest prophet that ever lived? Matthew 11:11 "Verily I say unto you, among them that are born of women there hath not risen a greater than John the Baptist: notwithstanding he that is least in the kingdom of heaven is greater than he." What an honor given to John the Baptist from the Savior!

> For I say unto you, among those that are born of women there is not a greater prophet than John the Baptist: but he that is least in the kingdom of God is greater than he. (Luke 7:28, KJV)

When we think of the preachers of the Old Testament, we usually think of the prophets, Elijah, Isaiah, Jonah, and others. Although the word "priest" is still in use for a segment of clergy among certain Christian churches (i.e. Catholic, Lutheran, etc.), in the evangelical ranks most ministers would not equate themselves in the same type of ministry. A priest might still be considered one who for the most part functions in a ceremonial role. Their pulpit ministries are not usually as pronounced as the Bible thumping preachers known in many of the evangelical churches.

In the Old Testament you can see a similar distinction between priest and prophet. Moses was a prophet. Aaron was a priest. It is interesting that Moses complained about his lack of speech when asked by God to deliver his command to Pharaoh to let the Israelites leave Egypt—but Moses still did the talking, even though God had conceded to Moses by sending Aaron as his spokesman. As we see the roles develop in the life of Moses and Aaron, we can see that their religious duties were very different. Aaron and his sons were given all the garments and duties of ceremony, but Moses was the prophet-preacher-shepherd that most evangelical pastors of today pattern themselves after.

We note that Prophets like Moses and Elijah were often endued with great power. These two were miracle workers, although we can't see the same evidence with other prophets such as Jonah or even Isaiah. One thing we do know, however, is that these men were chosen by God, ordained by God, commissioned by God, and their lives were God controlled, often to extreme measures. For those preachers today who want to be prophets, let me say, it isn't always easy.

For one thing, these men often found themselves alone in their work. Moses actually was not alone in his work, but Jonah, Jeremiah, and others were usually ministering alone and without help. Moses not only had Aaron, but God gave him seventy elders to assist him (Numbers 11:25). Moses was alone on the mountain when he received the Ten Commandments, but his ministry was more than just that of the simple prophet. His ministry was also that of a shepherd. There is really a distinction between Moses as a prophet and Jonah as a prophet.

Moses was a type of Jesus Christ. Other prophets were like Jesus Christ in other ways, but John the Baptist was that prophet who more than any could be seen as one who would be the last of that special breed of prophet-preacher sometimes seen in the Old Testament. Whether facing down a king or proclaiming judgment and God's vengeance, there would never be another John the Baptist. These men did usually work alone. Yes, they had disciples. Elijah had Elisha and John had baptized disciples. But their ministry was to preach—not to pastor, nor even to evangelize. They were proclaimers of God's word. But the elements that are needed for the New Testament church were evangelizing, gathering, guarding, building—these were not the usual characteristics of the Old Testament prophets. Actually, you might say, they spent much of their ministry tearing down walls in preparation for a new building to be built upon a new foundation.

It is true however that there are New Testament Prophets. Listed in the ministries of the church in Ephesians 4:11, the "prophet" is one of the ministerial gifts listed among what is commonly known as the "fivefold ministry."

> And he gave some, apostles; and some, prophets; and some, evangelists; and some, pastors and teachers; 12 For the perfecting of the saints, for the work of the ministry, for the edifying of the body of Christ. (Ephesians 4:11)

After John the Baptist we do not see another prophet in ministry other than Jesus Christ until we get to the book of Acts. This does not mean they did not exist. Anna (Luke 2:36) was a prophetess who ministered in the temple. The prophet is a ministry included in the New Testament church and exist today. The first mention is in Acts the 11th chapter. Agabus is mentioned by name as a prophet, but the scripture tells us that there were several in the church at Jerusalem. We find Agabus "foretelling" the famine to come upon the church. In two instances, Acts 11:27 and Acts 21:11 we find Agabus foretelling future events.

For a time, the apostle Paul was a prophet or teacher according to Acts 13:1. Judas and Silas were called prophets in Acts 15:32. The prophet is listed in 1 Corinthians 12:28 among the ministerial spiritual gifts and in 1 Corinthians 14 as the predominate form of spiritual ministry.

But what exactly is the prophetic ministry? Does it differ from that of the Old Testament? The answer is yes. Whereas the Old Testament prophet acted as the primary spokesman for God during that time, the New Testament prophet is only one of several ministries. The prophetic ministry of the New Testament is pictured as a part of the ministry of the "body" of Christ and does not stand-alone. For this reason, the purpose has been changed.

There is still the "foretelling" aspect as we see in Agabus, but the gift of prophecy, which may be exercised either by the-prophet or as a communal gift is generally used for the purpose of "edification, exhortation, and comfort" (1 Corinthians 14:3). It is not generally used as a means of pronouncing judgment or declaring rebuke. We find that reproving and rebuking can be administered, but it is through the preaching of God's word with long suffering and teaching (2 Timothy 4:2)

CHAPTER 20

The Evangelist

There is little information on the evangelist in the scripture other than the example of Philip (Acts 21:8). The word "evangelist" simply means "a carrier of glad tidings." Easton's Bible Dictionary points out that Philip evidently did not have the authority of the apostles, the gift of prophecy, nor the responsibility of a pastoral ministry. It is evident that Philip's ministry was for time and place.

We see Philip first going into Samaria where he preached Christ to the "un-evangelized" (Acts 8:5–25). He did work miracles and signs, preached the gospel, and baptized believers. He evidently did not have the gift of laying on of hands for his converts to receive the gift of the Holy Ghost, or perhaps it was needful that Peter be involved in the first outpouring of the Holy Ghost in Samaria in order to fulfill his personal commission. In any case we know that this was not evident in his ministry at this time.

We then see Philip evangelizing a congregation of one—the eunuch of Ethiopia (Acts 8:26–40). Again, other than preaching the gospel and baptizing, then being transported away—the ministry of Philip was limited in scope to reaching a lost individual.

The major characteristic of the evangelistic ministry is in the message. The anointing was powerfully attached to the gospel as being preached by Philip. It possibly did not include all the "filler" of the teacher or other ministries that we will sometime see. One might say that Philip and true evangelist "specialize" in gospel preaching limited to the gospel. The death, burial, resurrection of Jesus Christ is the basis of the message.

Could it be that many home mission's churches are started by an evangelist who feels that he needs to be a pastor? I have talked to many men who started churches and over the years have stuck it out—some to reach a peak but stay with small congregations and no move of God. The majority of home missions works eventually change hands or often will even close because there is not a transition in ministry.

On the other hand, there are men who are "pastoring" churches who are truly evangelist, but because of God's blessings, they have men who have grown and added to his ministry and he continues to be an evangelist while assuming the title of pastor. Other men in the church actually do the work of pastoring. I believe one way to determine what kind of ministry a man actually has is to look at how it functions. Is there a preacher who is more adept at counseling the saints? He may be pastoral in ministry. Is there a preacher who is a tremendous soul winner and does not work one on one with the problems of saints? He may be an evangelist.

It is because preachers feel that they must assume the title of pastor to be validated in a church or a district that we have lost the true recognition of ministries. Sometimes, therefore, churches will experience tremendous turnover because a pastoral or teaching ministry is not supporting an excellent evangelistic ministry. Then we glow in the excitement of constant activity and think we are doing great, when the many souls who have come and gone are an indication that there is not balance. Of course, we then blame it on the ones who leave as being worldly, sinful, or unbelieving.

CHAPTER 21

The Pastor and Elders

The Elders of the Local Church

I am purposely including the sections on elders and pastors together because of the confusion that exist between the two. As I have said above, it is important to understand the distinction between ministerial calling, gift, function, of a pastor, and the "office" of an elder.

One may really wonder why it would seem that if elders are ordained by man, how is that God would put elders above the ministries that God has ordained. This would be like having man's hand above God's hand. The fact is that for the most part, men who fill the eldership more often than not will have one of the ministerial gifts. It is not specifically required according to 1st Timothy 5:17, but it happens for the most part.

However, God made a distinction between pastors and elders in keeping with his concept of inverted authority. The role of elder (also known as bishop) refers to the function of leadership in the church rather than the function of preaching. What must be said about church leadership and authority must be said in the context of the office of elder or bishop. What must be said about "preaching" must be said in the context of the fivefold ministry. This is a necessary distinction in order to maintain a fivefold (or four-fold) ministry that would otherwise be destroyed if the office and gift became one and the same—a fact that I submit is exactly the point of this entire discussion. Men would become administrators instead of ministers.

The Pastor

The word "pastor" was used in the Old Testament for religious leaders in Israel and this ministry did not change from the Old Testament to the New Testament. Of course, the men who were given the ministry in the New Testament were ordained of God to this ministry rather than ordained of man—but that was true of any of the other ministries mentioned. All of these ministerial gifts were imparted by God's spirit and those who obtained them were to be Holy Spirit filled and anointed.

Since we did not have a New Testament example to refer to, we have to look in the Old Testament to find the job description of a pastor. The word "pastor" came from the Greek *poimen*, which literally means "shepherd," or "feeder of the flock." The word in the Hebrew is *raa*, which means both *shepherd* and *companion*. First of all, both as the God of the Old Testament and as Jesus Christ in the New Testament, God reveals himself as the "Shepherd of Israel" (Psalm 80:1), and describes his work in Ezekiel 34:12–22:

> As a shepherd seeketh out his flock in the day that he is among his sheep that are scattered; so will I seek out my sheep, and will deliver them out of all places where they have been scattered in the cloudy and dark day. 13 And I will bring them out from the people, and gather them from the countries, and will bring them to their own land, and feed them upon the mountains of Israel by the rivers, and in all the inhabited places of the country. 14 I will feed them in a good pasture, and upon the high mountains of Israel shall their fold be: there shall they lie in a good fold, and in a fat pasture shall they feed upon the moun-

> tains of Israel. 15 I will feed my flock, and I will
> cause them to lie down, saith the Lord GOD. 16
> I will seek that which was lost, and bring again
> that which was driven away, and will bind up
> that which was broken, and will strengthen that
> which was sick: but I will destroy the fat and the
> strong; I will feed them with judgment.

The primary work of pastors is toward the saved. Although it appears that in Acts 20:28 the job description of an elder and pastor are the same, thus causing some to assert that an elder or pastor is the same, there are some differences in the real definition. Primarily the distinction is that "elder" or "bishop" refers to the office while "pastor" refers to the gift of service. Let me note some distinctions here:

- A pastor has received a spiritual gift from God and is ordained by God to that "gift." An elder is ordained by man to the elder's "office."
- A pastor is primarily for the sheep. An elder is for oversight of the local church, which includes both, saved and lost who are in the congregation.
- A pastor's primary duties include feeding, healing, seeking, and restoration of the sheep. It does not extend to evangelizing, administration, ruling, or dealing with the unsaved (although it does not exclude these in the function of a soul winning saint). But we are speaking of the specific functions of pastors. The style of ministry for the pastor to the sheep differs from the style of ministry of the evangelist to the unsaved.
- An elder does not specifically have to have a "pulpit" ministry. Although both feed the sheep, we note that 1 Timothy 5:17 indicates that there may be elders who "labor in the word and doctrine," and elders who do not. Otherwise the term, "especially they who labor in the word and doctrine" would not have indicated that there was a distinction.

- The job description for elders is one of ruling and over-sight, which includes working with all of the other ministries in the church. Apostles, pastors, teachers, prophets, and evangelist are all subject to the elders of the local church as to direction, rules, availability of the pulpit. The General Chairman of any organization does not have the liberty to determine at what time he will take the pulpit when visiting in a local church. An apostle or pastor from another church does not have the liberty to set the order of the service or times of the service for another local church

It is very important to make a distinction between the gift of pastoring, as a ministerial or spiritual "preaching" gift and the "office" of elder (also known as bishop), which though requiring spiritual men is not a ministerial function but rather as the "gift to rule" (Romans 12:8). Pastoring is one of the "preaching" gifts, while bishop or elder refers to a nonpreaching gift, as an administrative gift.

Bishops and Elders

One question that might be asked is if there is a difference between *bishop* from the Greek *episkopos* and *elder* from the Greek *presbyteros*. The occasion for the question arises as it has become a practice that a pastor or elder is elevated to a "senior" status when there is a change in leadership whereby an intermediate level of authority is positioned in the leadership structure of the church. At times the change happens as a part of "dynasty succession" where a son replaces the pastor father as the "pastor" of the church; or it happens as a new pastor begins to serve. However, the change in title or distinction is intended to create a senior office to which the second pastor is purposely subordinated. This provision retains the power and control structure of the original church pastor.

However, the practice of bishops being seen as senior elders has for centuries been a common practice and used in designation of a higher office within several forms of church government. As mentioned earlier, Barnes noted that the early church father, Jerome, acknowledged that the term elder and bishop were synonymous, but the decree to elevate one presbyter above all the rest was a later development. In his commentary Barnes writes,

> The word used here occurs in the New Testament only in the following places: Acts 20:28, translated "overseers;" and Philippians 1:1; 1 Timothy 3:2; Titus 1:7; 1 Peter 2:25, in each of which places it is rendered as "bishop." The word properly means an inspector, overseer, or guardian, and was given to the ministers of the gospel because they exercised this care over the churches or were appointed to oversee their interests. It is a term, therefore, which might be given to any of the officers of the churches and was originally equivalent to the term presbyter. It is evidently used in this sense here. It cannot be used to denote a diocesan bishop; or a bishop having the care of the churches in a large district of country, and of a superior rank to other ministers of the gospel, because the word is used here in the plural number, and it is in the highest degree improbable that there were dioceses in Philippi. It is clear, moreover, that they were the only officers of the church there except "deacons;" and the persons referred to, therefore, must have been those who were invested simply with the pastoral office. Thus, Jerome, one of the early fathers, says, respecting the word bishop: A presbyter is the same as a bishop. And until there arose divisions in religion, churches were governed by a common counsel of presbyters. But afterward, it was everywhere decreed, that one person, elected

from the presbyters, should be placed over the others.[98]

The original usage of the term bishop was synonymous with the office of elder, although the words had different denotations. The word Episkopos, or bishop, means overseer or superintendent and denotes the function and responsibility of the church leader. In both Philippians 1:1 and in 1 Timothy 3, "bishops and deacons" are identified as the two primary offices of church leadership and are in the plural. Paul interchanges the word "bishop" and "elder" in Titus 1:5–7, again in the plural. The meaning of bishop, that is one with oversight or overseer, is used in reference to "elder" in 1 Peter 5:1–2, and also in Acts 20:17–28, which indicates that bishop and elder were commonly used interchangeably in scripture.

The better term for the church overseer is "bishop" that denotes the purpose and function of those in leadership. This is the term used for the office to which the qualifications were given in 1 Timothy and the term used to denote the office in Philippians 1. The term "elder" or "presbyter" simply means one that is senior and used both for age and for office. The context for the use of "elder" most likely was a prescription for ordaining those that were deserving of respect because of age, rather than a reference to the functional meaning. The term "bishop," therefore, in the context of scripture, places the emphasis on the office, while the term "elder" places the emphasis on the person, as an elder deserving of respect accorded to fathers or those of senior status in life.

Adam Clark in his *Commentary On the Whole Bible* agrees that bishop and elder are interchangeable in terms of purpose, authority, and status? Adam Clarke writes,

> Elders (Greek: *presbyteros*) or overseers (Greek: *episkopos)* are two words for the same charge (or "office," see *Acts 20:17*; *Acts 20:28*; *Titus 1:5*;

---

98. Albert Barnes, "Philippians 1," *Barnes Notes on the New Testament*, Edited by Robert Frew, Wordsearch, Edition 12 (2014).

Titus 1:7). Besides the New Testament also mentions the ministry of deacons (Greek: *diaconos*). Read Acts 6. These are all ministries and duties which existed as proper offices among the different assemblies in the beginning. The Jews had always had elders (*Exodus 3:16*; *Ezra 10:14*; *Matthew 26:59*; *Acts 6:12*). This is why we do not read of any appointing of elders into Jewish-Christian churches, although they existed there as well (*Acts 11:30*; *Acts 15:6*).[99]

The original designations of "bishop" and "elder" were purposeful in identifying the character and purpose of leadership in church government but were not intended to create offices of status that elevated one elder over another elder, which was the latter result in the early church. In keeping with scripture, whether bishop or elder, the designation is always in the plural. Francis Sullivan writes,

The question whether the episcopate is of divine institution continues to divide the churches, even though Christian scholars from both sides agree that one does not find the threefold structure of ministry, with bishop [pastor] in each local church assisted by presbyters and deacons, in the New Testament. They agree rather that the historic episcopate was the development in the post New Testament period, from the local leadership of a college of presbyters, who were sometimes called bishops (episkpoi), to the leadership of a single bishop.[100]

[99.] Adam Clarke, "Notes on 1 Timothy," *Commentary on the Whole Bible*, Online Edition. Retrieved from https://www.studylight.org/commentaries/acc/1-timothy.html.

[100.] Francis S. Sullivan, *From Apostles to Bishops: The Development of the Episcopy in the Early Church* (Mahwah, New Jersey: The Newman Press, 2001), Religious, 217.

Sullivan further notes,

> Scholars differ on details, such as how soon the church at Rome was led by a "monarchical" bishop, but hardly any doubt that the church at Rome was led by a group of presbyters for at least part of the second century.

The practice continues today, whether in a Presbyterian polity, Episcopalian polity, or in autonomous church structures led by a single pastor. Whether terminology such as bishop, elder, or pastor is used, the issue is not defining the office or emphasizing the person—the issue is whether there is a leadership structure within the local church that is inconsistent with the Lord's intention of servant-leadership and inverted authority that was created by design. The plurality of bishops (elders) was intended to prevent the concept of "monarchical" leadership in the church.

Now I can imagine that I would have just stirred up some controversy, but I pray that we will be open to the Bible, as well as reasoning. If we insist that all other ministries be subject to the pastor (when we believe that the pastor is the head of the church), why shouldn't we conclude that all other ministries (apostles included) are subject to the elders—if we conclude the elders are the legitimate overseers of the church?

The fact is that we have elevated pastor (a gift) to the position of elder (an office) to the exclusion of the other ministries. Most men will not recognize any one who calls himself an apostle, and seldom do men want to choose any other title than that of pastor because they would invalidate their position as the head of their local church. This is how ministries as spiritual gifts have gone on the decline.

CHAPTER 22

Teacher

One of the most suppressed of all ministries in the church today is the teaching ministry. Since all elders are apt to teach, and all pastors think they can teach, and since teaching does not always have the appeal of the fiery preacher, there are many teachers who sit in limbo on church pews frustrated and wanting to share what God has given, but being limited by our view of who really is supposed to do all the preaching.

I have met quite a number of great teachers who left their local churches and sought out positions as pastors in order to be validated. Again, the evidence that there is a lack of ministerial balance in the church over all is the fact that the average apostolic church is small in number and lacking in the operation of spiritual gifts.

The common argument—well the sheep should always hear the shepherd's (pastor's) voice—as a reason why the pastor does 90 percent of the preaching, is simply not a good one. If the sheep are listening to Jesus Christ, as they should be, they are hearing The Pastor's voice. If all they hear 90 percent of the time is the preacher in the church that calls himself by the title of pastor—let me submit unto you, that there is a lot less hearing of the pastor's voice then should be. I have listened to a lot of preaching over 30 years. It has included lots of filler, lots of story-telling, and lots of opinion.

The average saint has very little good teaching, or at least there can a lot more. I have heard men make almost whole sermons on why beards are a sin. Now for a man to preach against beards is lying—and lying is a sin. I have heard of the fellow that preached from the passage of scripture in Matthew 24:17—"Let him which is on the housetop not come down"—the title of his message "Top Not Come Down," a sermon against the wearing of wigs.

Good teaching is indeed a gift. Brother C. L. Dees use to explain the difference between the body, soul, and spirit this way. The soul is the seat of emotion. As the psalmist David once said, "And my soul shall be joyful in the LORD: it shall rejoice in his salvation" (Psalm 35:9); And again, "As the hart panteth after the water brooks, so panteth my soul after thee, O God" (Psalm 42:1).

The spirit on the other hand is the seat of understanding. We are told in Paul's writing to the Corinthians, "For what man knoweth the things of a man save the spirit of man which is in him? Even so the things of God knoweth no man, but the Spirit of God" (1 Corinthians 2:11). The body is the gateway for the soul and spirit to experience the life of this world.

The evangelist generally ministers to the emotions of man when he deals with repentance and the hunger and thirst of a man's soul. The teacher deals with the spirit of man when he feeds the understanding. Some of the best teacher's in the apostolic church were "dry as corn shucks" when it came to delivery, but the word came across in a powerful way to give understanding and resulting change in lives.

Now it is often said that "pastor and teacher" may be one ministry. I cannot argue that possibility since we know that the work of pastoring is more to the sheep than to the sinner. If that is the case, then I can certainly point out that a church can have more than pastor in Acts 13:1—just one more proof against the concept of a single-pastor church.

CHAPTER 23

The Ministry of Women

Up to this point, the discussion has been about recognizing the fivefold ministry. At the same time, a major point of this discussion is how the lack of plural elder-ship in the church and the change in concept to single rule by one who has become known as "pastor" has resulted in several kinds of abuses. Earlier, I stated that one of the results of centralizing the ministry into one individual in the local church has been that others in order to be validated feel that they must also become "pastors." This can result in men or women stepping out of what might be inadvertently a restrictive environment to receive either the freedom to minister or the recognition of a minister. Unfortunately, the least restrictive way of doing this is to become what is commonly known as a "pastor." The common second alternative is to take the title "evangelist" and become a roving preacher.

Concerning this centralization of ministry—in reality there was a centralization of power, which then created an unhealthy focus on a single ministry. Most pastors are willing to share the ministry but not the power represented by the office of the pastor. The truth is, the authority and power in the local church is to be centralized in Jesus Christ, and manifested in multiple leaders, not just one. A fivefold ministry (multiple ministries) and a multiple elder-ship both have the same premise—there is one head, Jesus Christ.

Here is the reality, however. God did intend that ministry was to operate in an environment which must be subject to spiritual authorities. If we look at ministry in the context of a spiritual gift rather than an office, it is easier to understand how both men and women can be used in the fivefold ministry without violating some of the biblical instructions concerning the qualifications for elders or deacons.

The first spiritual authority is the Holy Spirit itself—that is Jesus Christ. Only Jesus Christ can equip and anoint someone in the ministry. It is the Spirit that operates through an individual, and that person must follow the leading, direction, and prompting of the spirit of God in the operation of the gift. This is basic and I would think there is really no disputing this fact.

One of the reasons why I am addressing this issue is that the Bible does support the fact that women may be exercised under the authority of the Spirit of God in the fivefold ministries, if we recognize those ministerial gifts in the context of "function" rather than in the position of an office. That is, she may receive one of the ministerial gifts and it is important that she has the freedom to operate in that gift within the environment of the church. The second spiritual authority, however, is the word of God, and it is the word of God that limits the authority of a woman, but not the ministry of a woman. Before I discuss this further, I will point out that the third authority in the church is the leadership represented by elders and deacons.

But let us talk about how these authorities relate to the operation of a woman in the fivefold ministry. The easiest of the ministries to identify in reference to women is that of prophetess. There are several women in the Old Testament referred to as prophetesses, including Deborah (Judges 4:4), Huldah (2 Kings 22:14), Noadiah (Nehemiah 6:14), and the sister of Moses, Miriam (Exodus 15:20). In the New Testament we find Anna the prophetess in the temple (Luke 2:36) and the four daughters of Philip the evangelist (Acts 21:9).

I admit it is much more difficult to specifically identify by function women operating in the other ministries. However, if we were to look at the work of an apostle, for example, that which we commonly know as a missionary, we might see that there are many women who operate in that gift then and now. For example, Aquila and Priscilla appear to have ministered together in the several examples given of them in scripture. They were always mentioned together, not separately, first as possible converts of Paul, but then as laborers in the gospel. Together they instructed Apollos concerning the truth of the gospel (Acts 18:26). Then they were mentioned together as being fellow helpers to Paul (Romans 16:3), and together as having a church in their house (1 Corinthians 16:19).

Other prominent women who were spoken of for their labors in the Lord, include Tryphena, Tryphosa, and Persis (Romans 16:12). One possible reference to a woman apostle (missionary) is that of Junia (Romans 16:7). According to the Jamieson, Faussett, and Brown commentary, Junia was either the wife or sister of Andronicus, and the expression "who are note among the apostles" was literally, "noted apostles." This was the translation later accepted by Chrysotome, Luther, Calvin, Bengel, Olshausen, Jowett, and others.

One big problem today however, is the numerous situations where women have decided to operate in the "function" of an elder, because they believe that is the appropriate place to minister as a pastor. First let me state that the pastoral ministry is one that is to the sheep, and as we read in Ezekiel 34:12–16, the ministry of the shepherd was to seek for, restore, heal, and feed the sheep. The spiritual guardianship of a shepherd is that of one who must be intimate with the needs of the sheep. Most often, I believe that gift is evident in the ability of one to counsel.

In the context of the ministry of "pastoring," it is not so unrealistic to have "youth pastors," "pastors to the elderly," "pastors to women." The most ridiculous statement ever made is that a church can only have one pastor. And a woman may pastor in the context of ministry. But this in reference to the ministry does not give women the "authority" to be an elder or ruler over an assembly.

The ministry of a woman to women is evident in the scriptures. I once heard a preacher explain that the last place a woman should go for counseling is to the "pastor" of the church. One way to avoid the pitfalls that happen to ministers getting caught in unhealthy counseling relationships is to follow some steps laid out in scripture.

The first place of counsel for a woman in the church is her husband if she has one. The man was given to be a woman's covering. In 1 Corinthians there is a scripture that has often been taken out of context.

> Let your women keep silence in the churches: for it is not permitted unto them to speak; but they are commanded to be under obedience, as also saith the law. And if they will learn anything let them ask their husbands at home: for it is a shame for women to speak in the church. (1 Corinthians 14:34–35, KJV)

Some have felt that this scripture was written because women were chattering too much and being unruly. We know that it could not mean that a woman cannot say anything because we read in 1 Corinthians 11:5 that a woman may pray and prophesy. It is verse 35 that gives us the clue—"And if they will learn any thing, let them ask their husbands at home." In order to protect the headship and priestly covering that a man must be to the home, God ordained that the married women should first go to her husband if there were questions concerning church matters. Take notice that this admonition is not one of Paul's opinions, but rather we then read in verse 37, "If any man think himself to be a prophet, or spiritual, let him acknowledge that the things I write unto you are the commandments of the Lord." This appears to be one of the commandments often overlooked in scripture considering that it is often not followed in our society today.

But what if a woman is not married or if her husband is not a spiritual man or is possibly a sinner away from God? What if the husband is part of the problem? The second place a woman should go for spiritual guidance is to the "elder women," or it might be said, a woman who has the pastoral ministry. The best source of family counseling for the women in the church is the woman who has a walk with God and may have the pastoral ministerial gift. In Titus 2:3–4, it says,

The aged women likewise, that they be in behaviour as becometh holiness, not false accusers, not given to much wine, teachers of good things; That they may teach the young women to be sober, to love their husbands, to love their children.

What of a Woman Pastor over a Local Church?

The most common excuse I have heard from women who "pastor," as to their taking that role is, "no man would answer the call." First, we must understand that when we refer to pastor in this context it means one who has become the ruler of the assembly. After all, this is the function given to elders. "Obey them that have the rule over you and submit yourselves, for they watch for your souls" (Hebrews 13:17). Also, "Let the elders that rule well be counted worthy of double honor" (1 Timothy 5:17). The function of eldership is that of ruling or overseeing the assembly. The qualifications of an elder as we read in 1 Timothy 3 include that of being a good ruler over his house and being the husband of one wife. If this was the only scripture in the Bible that speaks of a man as a leader of the home or the church, we would have a problem, but the Bible has several references to the order of authority in the home as well as in the church.

Since this book is not intended to deal specifically with family relationships, I will assume that the reader has most likely some knowledge concerning the story of creation, the admonitions for the husbands, wives, and children concerning their duties in relationship, and all the scriptures that state a husband should love their wives, and wives submit to their husbands. I won't go into those here because I don't want to frustrate our lady readers when more importantly, I am advocating for their freedom to minister.

However, the freedom to minister in the fivefold ministry is not the same thing as the authority to rule a congregation. In the very first part of this book, I have suggested that the definition of ministry has been lost because of the changes that have taken place by centralizing authority in one person in the church. Women should desire whole heartedly to minister but should not desire to become rulers in either the church or the home—otherwise they have stepped out of place with God's order.

I mentioned that most women pastors whom I have known have used the excuse that they became the pastor of the church because there wasn't a man making himself available for the job. As I see it, this sends a wrong message to the ladies who are members of the congregation. Let me explain.

In 1 Peter 3:1, the scripture read, "Likewise, ye wives, be in subjection to your own husbands; that if any obey not the word, they also may without the word be won by the conversation (behavior) of the wives." This passage of scripture instructs the godly woman on what to do about the husband who is a sinner or not obedient to the word of God. Since the Bible instructs the man to be a Godly leader and teacher to the home and the head of woman (1 Corinthians 11:3), what should a woman do if the man chooses not to accept that responsibility? Should they then conclude that "if the husband won't be the head of the house, then I will be the head of the house"? No! The scripture teaches that a woman must continue in subjection to the husband even if he is out of place.

When a woman pastors a church using the excuse that no man was willing to do it, she sends a message to the ladies in her congregation that they have the liberty to supplant the husband as the head of the home if he is not functioning as he should in that role. If a woman becomes a pastor (elder-ruler) for any reason, she has stepped out of God's word which has plainly laid out the qualifications for the elders of the church (1 Timothy 3).

It is important to understand that there is a difference between the spiritual gifts that equip someone in the fivefold ministry, and the office or function of elder. Whether a man or a woman, an individual may be used in the ministerial gift providing they are subject to the three spiritual authorities ordained by God—the spirit of God, the word of God, and the leadership of ordained elders.

CHAPTER 24

Restoration Leadership

I am aware that there are men in different organizations who will fight the concept of collegial eldership. I realize that time, and tradition, are always powerful forces against change. But we have already been warned by Jesus Christ that tradition can make the word of God of no effect (Mark 7:13, KJV). At the same time, we are told that the apostles passed down traditions (2 Thessalonians 3:6). The Bible is clear that there are ministerial gifts, where God ordains men to those ministries, and there is plural eldership, where men are ordained by men to the office of elder.

I once assisted a fine man in a church who made a statement to me that I have always remembered. He rebuked me for using the term "body ministry" in a sermon because it sounded too charismatic. In my discussion with him, he let me know that in a prior church he had taught heavily on spiritual gifts in order to get them operating in the church, but when they began to operate, they created problems and then he had to reverse course and limit their operation.

It is apparent to me that spiritual gifts can be abused. There is a potential for abuse in plural eldership. But we are seeing tremendous abuse in the single-pastor concept and either don't want to acknowledge it or want to minimize it. We have disowned the offices of apostle and prophet. We have degraded the gifts of evangelist and teacher to a second-tier ministry. We have exalted the pastoral ministry above the real pastor, who is Jesus Christ, who is above all other ministries.

We have invalidated the callings of the many to promote the few. (This is something that was also done by Diotrephes.)

The result is that we now have hundreds of organizations with hundreds of churches, and hundreds of ministers who cannot or will not work together for the kingdom of God. In many cities there are multiple churches that cannot get together. It is not that there doesn't need to be more than one preaching point or location for services. But men should be able to work together to oversee the corporate body of a city. Often there are several churches with very small congregations meeting in less than adequate facilities. If these churches could merge, they could reap the benefits of larger congregations and financial stability. But they don't because someone has to be "the pastor."

Very little relationship develops among the body of Christ in a local area. This should not be. The responsibility and the blame lie with men who have a nonbiblical concept of church government. I am appealing to men who will read the scripture and make it right. It isn't going to be easy. How do you divide the tithes? How do you divide the pulpit? How do you divide the authority? I submit that these issues are not hard to figure out if you know they are supposed to be done.

The Challenge of Restoration

The first steps toward any spiritual change are prayer and understanding. Prayer can impact our lives in two ways. First, it brings understanding from the Lord. Second, it brings direction (or wisdom) from the Lord. It is true that knowing what to do is not the same thing as knowing how to do it. The first is knowledge, the second, wisdom.

Of course, every minister, pastor, and elder should want both the understanding and the wisdom to be relative to God's holy word. Both requests are to be made with the desire to know how to apply God's word to the understanding of ministerial gifts and to the application of church government. That is the purpose of this book.

Before anything can be done, leadership must be convinced through the Word and the Spirit concerning the truths that I have just written. If what I have written is understood to be true, then I suggest the following steps be taken:

1. Evaluate the current condition of the ministry in the church. If you are the sole pastor of the church, you are the current elder. As the current elder, you have the responsibility to ordain other elders in the church. You may get the assistance of another local pastor (elder) or district official but note that experience has shown that there will be many who will not accept the idea of multiple-eldership. It may be something one has to do alone. Also note that when Moses selected elders, God imparted to them the like spirit of Moses. If one says, "I have no one qualified," then is it not one of the jobs of an elder and minister to bring others to that qualification? But I submit that for the majority of mature churches, chances are good that elders are there.

2. Begin to teach on eldership in the church. Like most changes, there will always be resistance unless there is understanding. People fear what they don't know. What is the goal? To expand the oversight? To expand the ministry? To grow the church? What did Paul say was the work of the ministry? "For the perfecting the saints, for the work of the ministry, for the edifying (building up) of the body of Christ" (Ephesians 4:11, KJV).

3. Begin to teach on the fivefold ministry. Every church should be promoting both hand (fivefold) and congregational (or body) ministries. I once had a saint say to me, "Brother Davis, could you teach on spiritual gifts? We need some meat." I replied, "Brother, if you will read that again, teaching on spiritual gifts was milk because Corinth couldn't receive meat." Understanding ministry should be basic to every Christian's understanding of God's principles of living for God and relationship in the church.

4. If you select elders, they should be of a similar spirit and mind, but don't try to select "yes" men. Consider the qualifications and ministry of a man. Home mission works are a little more difficult because there are often limitations to the availability of qualified individuals. I believe another biblical principle should be considered here, that a home mission church should be started by no less than two men. This was the Lord's method of sending. But if a current home mission work is working with a sole pastor and not a plural eldership, the pastor should be looking to disciple men for qualification and not allow himself to limit his vision to a single-pastor church. If a man does not have a vision of eldership, chances are there is the danger of "personal kingdom building." One of the purposes of this book is to bring us to the understanding that it is not God's will to have sole-pastor churches.

The whole reason for 1 Timothy 3 is to provide a guideline for the selection of elders. Let me comment that God never intended that elders were to be chosen by the congregation. The voting in of pastors is another inappropriate process often done by evangelical churches. It is ironic that there are some processes in the liberal churches that are still correct. The eldership of the local church is a matter of succession, not one in which the sheep choose the shepherd. In those cases, the elders are sent or selected by other elders (bishops). Scripturally, all elders were ordained by apostles or elders. Only deacons were selected by the congregation and ratified by the apostles, if indeed Acts 6 refers to the selection of deacons.

Note what the apostles said regarding the placing these deacons: "Wherefore brethren, look ye out [that is, the congregation is to select] among you seven men…whom we may appoint" (Acts 6:3). These seven were chosen by the congregation and ratified (appointed) by the apostles or elders. Most often, elders are ordained from among those of the fivefold ministry that are a part of the congregation of the local church, but only by apostles or existing elders within the church.

Remember, Jesus is the pastor. We must examine our attitude toward other ministers in the local church. Are we guilty of paying ourselves out of the tithes, but not paying the other ministers the same? Are we guilty of not allowing any others to "pastor"? Do we give remuneration to visiting ministers but not to ministers in the local church when we ask them to serve or labor? Doesn't this automatically annul their gift or indicate that we don't acknowledge their ministry as a gift? Act with caution when it comes to remunerations, tithing, or support. Please understand that there can be a distinction and monetary difference in support.

Concerning the above, remember that eldership and ministry are two different things. There may indeed be a difference in remuneration because elders are worthy of double honor, especially if they labor in the word and doctrine. Because most pastors are preaching elders, their double honor accounts for both their eldership and their ministry. Once eldership is working correctly, the decisions of remuneration and support will become a shared responsibility and the level of support should be equitable in accordance with the responsibility provided by the elder or ministry.

The Bible makes a distinction between preaching elders and nonpreaching elders. There are also preachers who are not elders at all. They have not been ordained to that position in a church. My objection is that failing to support a man's labor is minimizing his ministry in attitude. It is not the money that matters; it is the principle. When local ministers preach, see that they are rewarded for their labor.

Remember that the job of elders is to oversee or rule the church, not to "preach once in a while." Here will be the biggest problem, learning to relinquish authority. God never intended a single pastor to have sole authority in the church. There is not one example of such church government in the scriptures. Jesus did not start the church in Jerusalem in such a manner, nor did the apostle Paul endorse any such model. You do, however, have the authority to ordain elders. Then you must learn to work with other elders. Working together, a fivefold ministry will flourish and the church will flourish.

Quit using the titles pastor, apostle, or bishop as a senior elder over other elders. Every elder is a bishop (Titus 1:5–7). Bishops are not elders over other elders. How do you know you are a pastor? Why do you have to be a pastor? Could you be an evangelist? Quit telling people, "I am THE pastor." Only Jesus is THE PASTOR. You may be a pastor, but when you use such language, it assumes that there can be no other pastors in the church. This is totally incorrect. You may be THE ELDER if there are no other elders in the church, but hopefully it will not remain that way. If you are a pastor, you may say so in the context of your ministry, but you must understand what kind of ministry a pastor has. Never give any saint the impression that only a pastor can oversee a church.

Give recognition to all ministers of the gospel when you are able to do so in a meeting. If you are in charge of a service, refrain from only recognizing pastors. If you know that there are other ministries there, recognize them all. This includes teachers, apostles, evangelist, prophets, those who have worked as assistant pastors. Otherwise, just recognize all the preachers and elders regardless of which ministry they may have.

Change the by-laws of the church to allow for eldership. This allows for succession and continuity from within the church. If the church needs a pastoral ministry, then let the elders seek a pastor to add to the eldership. If the church needs an evangelistic ministry, let the elders seek an evangelist. But the eldership must recognize one another's ministries and give freedom to those styles of ministry.

If a church is small and there is another church of the same faith in the local area, cannot churches consolidate and have elders that work together? I can understand how this is not likely to happen unless both pastors come to the same conclusion. You can have more than one pastor and share eldership. But to have two or more churches of the same faith right near each other is a shame to the Kingdom of God. It creates division among the brotherhood. Such things should never be.

I can picture some now saying, "Oh no, the church is being run by the elders." Is that not what the Bible teaches? "Let the elders that rule well..." "Obey them [plural] that have the rule over you..."

What is the difference between being ruled by one and being ruled by many? With plural eldership, no one person can become the focus. If the eldership is doing what it should, there should be no focus on any single individual but on Jesus Christ alone. If the eldership is doing what is should be doing, multiple ministries, the fivefold ministry, should flourish.

A Conclusion: First among Equals

I conclude with one caveat. The Bible does not mention senior pastors and assistant pastors. One of our practical and legitimate questions concerns whether or not members of the collegial eldership would all have equal voice or responsibility. What about the idea that the pulpit would be shared equally among all elders when the Bible indicates that there are elders who labor in the word and doctrine? This of course would imply that there are elders who do not labor in the word in doctrine (pulpit preachers, so to speak). It should be obvious that the pulpit would not be equally shared, and it is also obvious for that reason that there was a double honor or distinction in reward.

In practice, when one elder ordains another, the new elder takes responsibility and oversight of the church in equality with the first elder. But it can also be noted that, while the apostles were equal in order, Jesus shared with three notables in an inner circle. These were Peter, James, and John.

As the church was established at Jerusalem, we notice that the apostles were in conference with elders who now had their voices. All the decrees to the churches did not come from the apostles alone. But the Bible also alludes to James, the brother of Jesus, as being a chief spokesman. Some want to conclude from this that James was "the pastor" of the church in Jerusalem, but that would be in contradiction to all the other scriptures that teach the church is to be overseen by elders.

Paul writes in Galatians 2:9 that Peter, James, and John "seemed to be pillars," and it was his impression that there was significance in how these three viewed the ministry of Paul and Barnabas.

In all of this, let it be said that it is not likely that Peter, James, or John ever took the opportunity to elevate themselves in their offices. After all, it was John and his brother James (not Jesus's brother) who were rebuked for desiring a place on the right and left hand of Jesus's throne. It was these two who reaped the indignation of the other ten when Jesus first explained his principle of authority inverted, which I mentioned in the first chapter of this book.

I believe that most men who are now pastors of churches are humbly trying to do the right thing. Unfortunately, they're trying to do the right thing the wrong way. I pray that a study of scripture and consideration of these things written will at least create a desire to see a restored fivefold ministry.

BIBLIOGRAPHY

Adkins, Amy, "B2B Organic Growth Demands a Strong Organizational Identity." *Gallup Business Journal*, April 19, 2016. Business Collection (accessed March 15, 2019). http://link.galegroup.com/apps/doc/A451263651/GPS?u=fl_program&sid=GPS&xid=e5a85ef9.

Bandura, Albert. (1997). *Self Efficacy—The Exercise of Control.* (New York, NY: W. H. Freeman and Company, 1997), 6.

Barnes, Albert. "Philippians 1," *Barnes Notes on the New Testament,* Edited by Robert Frew, Wordsearch, Edition 12, (2014)

Barrett, David B., Kurian, George T., Johnson, Todd, M. *The World Christian Encyclopedia: A Comparative Survey of Churches and Religions in the Modern World (2nd Edition).* Oxford, New York: Oxford University Press, 2001

Benzel, David. "Build credibility: shed the superman cape." *Leadership Excellence,* 25, 1 (Jan 2008), pp. 12–14. Retrieved July 2, 2009 from Business Source Complete database: Liberty University.

Block, Stephen. R., and Rosenberg, Steven. "Toward an understanding of founder's syndrome." *Nonprofit Management & Leadership 12,* no. 4, (2002), 353–368. Retrieved from https://tinyurl.com/y65joe67

Bolman, Lee G. & Deal, Terrance, E. "Reframing Leadership." In J. V. Gallos (Ed.). *Business Leadership* (pp. 35–49). San Francisco: Jossey-Bass, 2008.

Boone, Larry W. & Makhani, Sanya. "Five necessary attitudes of a servant leader." *Review of Business, 33* (1), (2002, Winter), 83–96.

Butler, Diana H. Standing against the Whirlwind: Evangelical Episcopalians in Nineteenth-Century America. New York: New York: Oxford University Press, 1995.

Cashman, Kevin. (2008). "Energetic Leadership." *Leadership Excellence,* 25, 10 (October 2008):16. Retrieved July 20, 2009 from Business Source Complete: Liberty University.

Cassell, J. & Hold, T. The servant leader. American School Board Journal, 195, 10 (October 2008): 34–35. Retrieved July 18, 2009 from Academic Source Complete: Liberty University.

Chute, Anthony. "Baptist Foundations: Church Government for an Anti-institutional Age." *Baptist History and Heritage* 51, no. 2 (2016): 94+. General OneFile (accessed March 15, 2019). https://link.galegroup.com/apps/doc/A468140934/GPS?u=fl_program&sid=GPS&xid=4b71fe31.

Clarke, Adam. "Notes on 1 Timothy," *Commentary on the Whole Bible,* Online Edition. Retrieved from https://www.studylight.org/commentaries/acc/1-timothy.html

Collins, D. B., & Holton, E. F. (2004). The Effectiveness of Managerial Leadership Development Programs: A Meta-analysis of Studies from 1982 to 2001. Human Resource Development Quarterly, 15 (2), 232.

Colson, Charles. & Larson, Catherine. "The lost art of commitment." *Christianity Today,* 54, (8) (2010) p. 49.

Cramm, Susan. "When you're a leader, everyone is watching you." *CIO,* (December 15, 2007), 21, 6, pp. 32–34. Retrieved July 17, 2009 EBSCOhost, doi:Susan Cramm.

Damazio, Frank. *The Making of a Leader.* Portland, OR: City Bible Publishing, 1988

Davis, Alan. "Authentic leadership: future proofing your organization's reputation." *Human Resources Magazine,* June/July 2009, 14, 2, p. 1. Retrieved July 17, 2009 from Business Source Complete: Liberty University.

Davis, Hartwell T. Paul. *Restoring the Fivefold Ministry.* Coral Springs, FL: Llumina Press (2004)

Davis, Hartwell T. Paul. "The Called, Chosen, and Faithful Leader." *Educations Resources Information Center, (2009).* Retrieved from https://eric.ed.gov/?q=Hartwell+Davis&id=ED506263

Davis, Hartwell T. Paul. "Reframing Leadership" (Book review), 2009. Liberty University: An Essay Presented in Graduate Studies

Davis, Hartwell T. Paul. "Discipleship Methods: Commitment and Loyalty as First Principles of Leadership Development" (2014). Regent University: An Essay for Organizational Leadership

Davis, Hartwell T. Paul. "Power Structures in the Configuration of Servant Leadership" (2015). Regent University: Essay for Organizational Leadership

Delbecq, Andre L. "Nourishing the Soul of the Leader." *Business Leadership*. Ed. J. V. Gallos. San Francisco: Jossey-Bass, 2008. 180–198

DeSilva, David A. *An Introduction to the New Testament: Contexts, Methods, and Ministry Formation*. Downers Grove, IL: Inter Varsity Press (2004), 757

De Vita, Emma. "Servant-Leadership." *Third Sector*, (24 September 2008) p. 25. https://www.thirdsector.co.uk/theory-servant-lead ership/communications/article/848028

Dogan, Mattei. "Introduction: Diversity of Elite Configurations and Clusters of Power." *Comparative Sociology*, 2 (1), (2003), 1.

Eadie, John. *The Ecclesiastical Cyclopaedia 5th ed*. London, United Kingdom: Charles Griffin and Company, January 1, 1875, 512

Eddleman, Kirk. "Founder's Syndrome: Most Frequently Seen in Entrepreneurial Practices, This Condition Can Cripple Your Performance." EQUUS, (404), S12, May 2011. Retrieved from http://link.galegroup.com/apps/doc/A255492952/GPS?u=fl _program&sid=GPS&xid=a27b29e0

Evans, Justin J. "The Facts and Stats on 33,000 Denominations." Gordon-Corwell Theological Seminary, http://www.philvaz. com/apologetics/a106.htm.

Friend, Celeste. (n.d.). "Social contract theory." *Internet Encyclopedia of Philosophy*. Retrieved from https://www.iep.utm.edu/soc-cont/

Gallos, Joan. (2008). *Business Leadership* (pp. 180–198). San Francisco: Jossey-Bass.

Grady, J. Lee, "The other Pentecostals." *Charisma Magazine*. Orlando, Florida: Charisma, June, 1967, 62–63.

Graham, Ross. "The Biblical Origins of the Presbytery." *Ordained Servant, 5, no. 2.* (Willow Grove, PA: The Orthodox Presbyterian Church, 1996). Retrieved from https://www.opc.org/OS/html/V5/2f.html

Harder, Leland. "The Concept of Discipleship in Christian Education." *Religious Education, 58 (4)(1963) 347–358.*

Hatch, Mary J., & Cunliffe, Ann L. *Organization Theory: Modern, Symbolic, and Postmodern Perspectives.* (2nd ed.). Oxford, NY: Oxford University Press, 2006.

Herrick, Greg. "Understanding the Meaning of the Term Disciple." *Bible.org, Series Go Make Disciples of All Nations, (2),* 11 May 2004. Retrieved from https://bible.org/seriespage/2-understanding-meaning-term-disciple

Huizing, Russell L. "Leaders From Disciples: The Church's Contribution To Leadership Development." *Evangelical Review of Theology, 35,* 4, October 2011.

Kalin, Sally W. "Reframing Leadership: The ACRL/Harvard Leadership Institute for Academic Librarians." *Journal of Business & Finance Librarianship*, 13, 3, (April 29, 2009), 261–270. Retrieved June 15, 2009 https://www.tandfonline.com/doi/abs/10.1080/08963560802183047

Keith, Kent M. "Servant leaders: Observe Three Basic Principles." *Leadership Excellence*, 26, 5, (May 2009) 18–19. Retrieved July 18, 2009 from Business Source Complete.

"Kongo Gumi Construction." *Businesses Today* (November 29, 2011). https://businessestoday.wordpress.com/tag/kongo-gumi-construction/

Lindsey, Thomas M. (1939). "Ministry." In *International Standard Bible Encyclopedia, edited by James Orr.* Grand Rapids, MI: William B. Eerdmans Publishing

Long, Stephen. "Executive Presence: What Is It and How to Get It." Nonprofit World 29, no. 6 (Nov/Dec 2011): 14–15. Retrieved from https://search-proquest-com.ezproxy.liberty.edu/docview/928448770?accountid=12085.

Marak, George E. Jr. "The Evolution of Leadership Structure. Sociometry, 27, (2), (June 1964), 175. Retrieved from https://www.jstor.org/stable/2785714

Maxwell, John C & Elmore, Tim. *The Maxwell Leadership Bible* (2nd Ed.). Nashville, TN: Thomas Nelson, 2007.

McGlone, Lee (1989). *Review and Expositor, 86,* p. 244.

Milco, Michael R. *Ethical Dilemmas in Church Leadership: Case Studies in Biblical Decision Making (Kindle ed.).* Grand Rapids, MI: Kregel Publications, 1997.

Milliman, John, PhD. and Jeffery Ferguson PhD. "In Search of the 'Spiritual'" in Spiritual Leadership: A Case Study of Entrepreneur Steve Bigari. *"Business Renaissance Quarterly 3,"* no. 1 (Spring, 2008): 19–40, http://ezproxy.liberty.edu/login?url=https://search-proquest-com.ezproxy.liberty.edu/docview/212540603?accountid=12085.

"Ministry," in International Standard Bible Encyclopedia, Electronic Database, Biblesoft, 1996

Padony, Joel M. "The Buck Stops and Starts at Business School." *Harvard Business Review,* (June 2009). Retrieved from https://hbr.org/2009/06/the-buck-stops-and-starts-at-business-school

Power (n.d.) *Online Etymology Dictionary.* Retrieved from http://www.etymonline.com/index.php?term=power

Rawson, Hugh. "Some Rules Aren't Made To Be Broken." In *The Daily Telegraph,* (August 26, 2008), Features, p. 16. Retrieved July 18, 2009 https://www.telegraph.co.uk/news/features/3637804/Some-rules-arent-made-to-be-broken.html

"Rightly or wrongly, people judge each other by the way they look. But what happens if these judgments affect their job prospects or the advancement of their career?" *Estates Gazette,* July 21, 2012. Business Collection (accessed March 19, 2019). http://link.galegroup.com/apps/doc/A297482386/GPS?u=fl_program&sid=GPS&xid=0a3a6030.

Robbins, Stephen P. & Judge, Timothy A. *Organizational Behavior (13th Ed.).* Upper Saddle River, NJ: Prentice-Hall, 2009.

Saad, Lydia. "Congressional Approval Hits Record Low 14%." *Gallup Poll Briefing* (July 16, 2008), 1. Retrieved July 18, 2009 from Business Source Complete: Liberty University.

Sales, Michael J. "Leadership and the Power of Position." In Joan V. Gallos (Ed.), *Business Leadership*. San Francisco: Jossey-Bass, 2008, 180–198.

Salvatore, Gabriella. "Develop Tomorrow's Leaders." *Training*, 46, 5 (June 2009), 38. Retrieved July 13, 2009 from Business Source Complete: Liberty University.

Sample, Steven B. "Thinking Gray and Free." In Joan V. Gallos (Ed.), *Business Leadership* (pp. 115–124). San Francisco: Jossey-Bass, 2008.

Sullivan, Francis A. *From Apostles to Bishops: The Development of the Episcopy in the Early Church*. Mahwah, New Jersey: The Newman Press, 2001. Religious.

Sullivan, James. "Studying Mistakes with Humility, Discipline Reveals the Lessons That Make Great Leaders." *Nation's Restaurant News*, 43, 21, (June 8, 2009): 14–50. Retrieved July 20, 2009 from Business Source Complete

Trichinotis, M. & Scheiner, G. "Committed Leadership: Going for the Gold." *Armed Forces Comptroller*, 41, no. 4 (1996) 39. Retrieved July 15, 2009 from Business Source Complete.

Vorster, Nico. "Are Freedom and Equality Natural Enemies? A Christian Theological Perspective." *Heythrop Journal*, 51 (4), 2010, 594–609.

Wheeler, David A. "Introduction to Servant Evangelism." *Liberty University*. Course taken January 2010

Williams, Charles. *Effective Management, 5th Edition*. Mason, OH: South-Western Cengage, 2012.

Zenger, John H. & Folkman, Joseph. "Ten Fatal Flaws That Derail Leaders." *Harvard Business Review*, 87, 6 (June 2009), 18. Retrieved July 20, 2009 from Business Source Complete

ABOUT THE AUTHOR

Hartwell Paul Davis has a postgraduate degree in teaching and curriculum from Liberty University; a masters in management and leadership, also from Liberty; and doctoral studies in organizational leadership from Regent University. For the past ten years, he has been a professor of English, psychology, and business at several universities in Florida. Paul Davis has for forty-five years been a church planter, having started churches in New York, Rhode Island, Virginia, Pennsylvania, South Carolina, and Florida. His many years' experience in business, social work, and church planting provide a rich background for his secular and pastoral work over the past forty-five years. He now lives in Florida with his wife, Diane, who is of Jewish heritage and considers herself a "completed Jew," but in retirement he continues to be actively involved in church work and ministry.

CPSIA information can be obtained
at www.ICGtesting.com
Printed in the USA
FSHW012019250919
62392FS